Fly Fishing the

MW01027794

Olympic Peninsula

Doug Rose

"After a little coaxing, I can usually get the locals to reveal a decent stretch of water off the beaten path where I can walk in and enjoy the quiet. I'll study the river a long time, imagining the people who fish it and realizing this river means as much to them as the Lost does to my family."

"The Sky Fisherman"
by Craig Lesley

About the Author

Doug Rose is a freelance outdoor writer and journalist specializing in fishing, hunting, hiking and natural resource management issues. His articles on the Olympic Peninsula fishing have appeared in *Salmon Trout Steelheader*, *Fly Fisherman*, *Game & Fish* and other regional and national publications. His writing experiences include staff positions as a government reporter and feature writer for newspapers in Washington and Oregon. He currently writes the "Great Outdoors" column in the *Port Townsend Jefferson County Leader*. He and his wife, Lisa are the resident caretakers of the Dungeness National Wildlife Refuge on the Olympic Peninsula's north coast.

This book is dedicated to Lisa who was there every step of the way.

© **1996 by Doug Rose**

All rights reserved. No part of this book may be reproduced without the express written consent of the publisher, except in the case of brief excerpts in critical reviews and articles.

All inquiries should be addressed to:
Frank Amato Publications, Inc.
P.O. Box 82112, Portland, Oregon 97282

Book Design and Layout: Alan Reid
Photos: Doug Rose unless otherwise noted

Softbound ISBN: 1-57188-099-2
UPC: 0-66066-00293-8

Printed in Canada
1   3   5   7   9   10   8   6   4   2

Table of Contents

I am swinging a Polar Shrimp Spey on the Hoh River in Olympic National Park.

It is early October, a time of blue skies and low water in this, the oozing, moss-draped northwest corner of the country. The day before, I hiked upriver from the Hoh Rain Forest Visitor Center and pitched my tent in a grove of 200-foot-tall Sitka spruce. Despite the dry weather, the sun sets early in October this far north, especially when there is a 1,000-foot ridge to the south of the river. By the time I finished making camp, I had a choice: fish for 20 minutes or gather firewood. Knowing that the autumn twilight would be short and the rain forest night long, I gathered firewood.

It is morning now. I have just tossed two loose upstream mends to slow my wet-fly swing. Down at the end of my short, four-foot leader, out of sight in the Hoh's glacial green water, I can feel the soft pulse of my fly.

I am fishing for steelhead, summer steelhead. The Hoh is best known as a winter steelhead river. But it also supports a modest run of summer steelhead, both natives and a rather significant number of hatchery "dip ins" from other rivers. By October, the slender, narrow-waisted Hoh natives have negotiated the 30 miles from the mouth up to the small pools, pocket water and creek mouths of the Hoh backcountry. Each autumn, I grab my old Kelty pack and head up the Hoh River Trail.

A restless brawling ribbon of jade, the Hoh heads up on glaciers and snowfields on the slopes of Mount Olympus, at 7,965 feet, the Olympic Peninsula's loftiest peak. On its journey from the Ice Age landscape of the high country to the gray breakers of the Pacific Ocean, the Hoh winds through one of the most unusual and remote areas of the lower 48 states—the Hoh Rain Forest. Here, nourished by 12 feet of rain a year and a climate where freezing temperatures are rare and summertime fog keeps the forest cool, vegetation not only thrives—it explodes. From the crowns of Sitka spruce to the clover-like carpet of wood sorrel on the forest floor, and from the draperies of club moss on big leaf maple to the lacy filagree of its fern and huckleberry understory, the rain forest is a riot of green.

As my fly completes its swing, I strip line in cautiously, then take two steps downstream and cast again. To an observer, the downstream wet-fly swing—cast, mend, swing, retrieve, two steps down—probably looks like a metronomyc way of fishing. And there are more fashionable methods of fishing for summer steelhead. But the greased line, the riffling hitch, waking and skating all work better on slower and clearer rivers than the Hoh. Besides, the wet-fly swing requires concentration because the strike of a steelhead, even a summer-run, is often little more than a momentary hesitation, a slight tick in the rhythm of the swing.

Summer steelhead aren't the only fish in this part of the river in October. I have taken small, jewel-like resident rainbows, Dolly Varden/bull trout and whitefish from the pool just upstream. Brawny Chinook salmon, their flanks the deep ochre of their spawning colors, often hug the soft water in the deepest part of the pool this time of year. Coho salmon rest briefly above the tailout on their journey to the creek mouths where they will spawn in early winter. And crimson-spotted anadromous char, some pushing eight pounds, hang in the slack water outside the main flow, looking for drifting salmon eggs or a hapless sculpin.

Still, it is summer steelhead that I am after. And as I strip my line in once again, my mind wanders to other summer-runs I have taken from the pool. I think of the chrome-bright 10-pounder I took under a bright sun two years ago. I remember the dazzling acrobatics of the seven-pounder last October.

Taking two more steps downstream, I cast again. My fly lands about six feet above the spot where the tailout picks up speed and empties into a 100-yard-long run. This is the best water in the entire pool, the place where I anticipate a fish on every cast.

Suddenly, I hear the shrill whistle of a bugling bull elk. For me, Roosevelt elk are as integral a part of my October trips as the steelhead themselves. But rutting elk had kept me awake half the night. A bull had thrashed brush and bugled so closely to my tent that I could hear the low, rattling chest-cavity rumble at the conclusion of its bugle. The cows spent much of the night racing back and forth across the glade, their hooves dull thuds on the spongy rain forest floor. Elk aren't menacing creatures, but I didn't want to be stepped on by an 800-pound animal in the transports of autumnal passion, either. By morning, I was, shall we say, sensitized to elk.

Looking downstream now, I see a mature bull wading the downstream end of the long run below the tailout. Its back is caked with mud and vegetation hangs from its antlers. Courting attire. It steps off the bar and wades to the far side of the river. Daylight has restored my equanimity about elk, and I am absorbed by its purposeful gait and the glint of sunlight on its antler tips.

Just then, a sharp tap telegraphs up the length of my fly line. I swing the rod back quickly, but don't feel anything. Damn, I think, I should have been paying attention. But then a steelhead thrashes on the surface. I jerk back sharply on the rod again. This time, there is the heavy throb of a fish.

Feeling the hook, the fish streaks downstream, then jumps. It jumps a second time, clearing the water in an iridescent halo of spray. Then it thrashes on the surface. When I try to put a little pressure on it with the rod, it shakes its head angrily and races back upstream to the pool.

In the clear autumn water, I can see the steelhead rubbing the hook on the river bottom. I gently lever the rod back and forth and crank the reel handle. I regain a few feet of line, but every third or fourth pull the fish runs back out into the main current.

"Come on baby," I say. "Come on now."

The battle seesaws back and forth for awhile. But at some point it occurs to me that I am past that hell's-a-popping, out-of-control part of the fight where anything can happen. I am aware that I will probably land the fish. When I try to lead it toward a sandy, level section of the bar, however, it spooks and dashes back into the current. This happens three times before I finally can reach down and grab the fish between its tail fin and body.

It is a beautiful fish, a 10-pound native Hoh summer steelhead. Its back has taken on the green tint of a resident rainbow and there are splashes of rose on its gill plates and sides, signs that it has been in the river for a while. It thrashes briefly, then quiets. The barbless fly slips easily from the hinge of its jaw. I cradle the fish in my palms, working it slowly back and forth in the current. It is free but doesn't realize it. Then it shudders several times. It disappears into the lime-pulp green wash of the Hoh.

"Alright," I say, as I splash out of the shallows. "Alright."

On impulse, I look downstream. The bull elk is gone. But two cows and a yearling are wading the river, following it up into the trees.

In most parts of the country, a 50-mile-long river flowing through country so remote there is not even a town along it would be a treasure. Similarly, a watershed supporting healthy populations of four species of salmon, two species of migratory trout and resident and anadromous char would be heralded as an ecological miracle in many regions of the United States. And regardless of where you are from, a river that remains open to sport fishing eleven-and-one-half months a year and that, moreover, holds the reasonable promise of 10-, 15- and 20-pound fish on the fly would seem to be more the stuff of fantasies than a palpable, mossy-smelling reality.

Yet the Hoh is all of these things. Perhaps even more remarkable, however, is the fact that in the 1,400-square-mile region of glacier-clad mountains, ancient forests and fog-bound shorelines known as the Olympic Peninsula, the Hoh, though celebrated, is not particularly unique. Just one watershed to the south, for example, the native winter steelhead on the Queets River run even larger, and its river valley is even more remote than the Hoh's. Several ridgelines to the north, the Sol Duc River not only supports all five species of North American Pacific salmon, winter and summer steelhead, cutthroat and Dolly Varden/bull trout—it also has the grace to stay in shape for fly fishing during all but the most torrential downpours.

All in all, more than a dozen major rivers—the Dosewallips, Duckabush, Hamma Hamma and Skokomish on the east; the Satsop, Wynoochee, and Humptulips on the south; the Quinault, Queets, Hoh, Bogachiel, Calawah and Sol Duc on the west; and the Elwha and Dungeness on the north—radiate out to tidewater from the peninsula's mountainous interior. And each of these systems hosts combinations of migratory fish that are unique chronologically, spatially and physically. Sol Duc coho begin to nose up from tidewater in August, for example, while bright silvers still enter the Satsop in January. In addition to the large systems, virtually every tanin-stained cedar creek and chattering freestone stream supports a population of sea-run cutthroat, with many supporting modest runs of winter steelhead and salmon as well.

And that is just the rivers. From sprawling Lake Ozette's cutthroat to fjord-like Lake Crescent's unique 15-pound Beardslee rainbow, and from the sparkling subalpine tarns of the Buckhorn, Brothers and Mount Skokomish Wilderness Areas to the murky beaver ponds of Hood Canal's lowlands, the Olympic Peninsula offers a stillwater fly fishing experience for every mood and every season. Moreover, in a region besotted of anadromous fish, where the conventional (and generally most effective) angling strategy consists of letting the current swing a wet fly down- and across-stream, the trout in Olympic lakes allow fly fishermen to play around with the fly fishing techniques and strategies that are the cornerstones of the sport in other parts of the country—matching the hatch, nymph fishing, trolling flies.

Finally, surrounded on the west by the Pacific Ocean, the north by the Strait of Juan de Fuca and the east by Hood Canal, the Olympic Peninsula also presents fly fishermen with an all-but-untapped inshore saltwater fishery. Indeed, until quite recently, the rockfish, greenling, surfperch and flatfish of the peninsula's saltwater beaches were ignored by fishermen in general, and fly fishermen in particular. With the decline in salmon runs this has changed somewhat. Even so, the overwhelming majority of saltwater fishermen concentrate on the large offshore species—lingcod, halibut and the larger rockfish. Meanwhile, marine and anadromous fish still abound off the peninsula's rocky coast, along its sandy beaches and over the clam flats and oyster bars of its estuaries. Of all the Olympic fisheries, nearshore saltwater fishing holds the most promise for innovative anglers—for the technically gifted fishermen who develop hybrid lines and fly patterns and for the observant angler-naturalists who chart the seasons and tides of the peninsula's saltwater fish.

With the vaguely concentric Olympic Mountains channeling the weather systems off the North Pacific into dozens of microclimates, the Olympic Peninsula also contains more varieties of scenery and habitat than any other location on the West Coast.

Rain shadow valleys on the leeward side of the mountains, which receive as little as 15 inches of rain a year, support plant communities more commonly associated with California than western Washington. Yet less than 30 miles across the mountains, the 200 inches of precipitation a year that fall on the headwaters of the Hoh, Queets and Quinault rivers maintains the lowest-elevation glacier complex in the country and the Northern Hemisphere's most spectacular rain forest valleys. In between these extremes, the Olympics offer fly fishing settings for every season and every sensibility.

Despite the diversity, year-round availability and sheer abundance of Olympic fish, fly fishermen have been few and far between on the Olympic Peninsula until recently. Oh sure, there have been exceptions, notable, glorious exceptions. Syd Glasso, widely heralded as the father of the American Spey fly, lived and successfully fished the Quillayute rivers and the Hoh for summer and winter steelhead in the 1950s and 1960s. And, during the 1970s and 1980s, Jim Garrett a Washington Department of Fisheries employee, developed an exquisitely-detailed series of stonefly nymphs for steelhead and sea-run cutthroat, as well as flies for the peninsula's salmon. Because of these men's efforts, it is now possible to fill a fly box with patterns originated on the Olympic Peninsula. But Glasso and Garrett were the exceptions, men of passion and discipline, anchorites in a desert of bait fishermen, plug pullers and hardware slingers.

Why, you may wonder, did it take so long for fly fishing to take hold on the peninsula? Well, the most compelling reason is simple: It's a tough place to fish. The Olympic Peninsula has the tallest mountains, the deepest canyons and the most impenetrable forests on the Pacific Coast. Many of the better fishing areas are only accessible after a strenuous hike. Moreover, the roadside rivers are cold, steep and fast, which tended to discourage early fly fishermen. And until the last few years fly fishing

services—knowledgeable guides, fly shops with reliable information on the species and insects—have been non-existent. Even today, most successful Olympic Peninsula fly fishermen are highly independent specialists who almost never run into each other.

For many, perhaps most, fly fishermen, the kind of angling I have just described isn't very appealing. Indeed, a great number of fishermen enjoy the conviviality of waiting their turn at a celebrated pool. They enjoy the friendly competition and the knowledge that decades of other fishermen have also waded the same water. These anglers are usually happiest on rivers where the pools all have names, and lakes where the hatches have become codified to the point that you can pick up a tip sheet at the nearby fly shop. If you like this type of fly fishing, you will hate the Olympic Peninsula.

But if you can read water and don't mind walking you can connect with large, wild fish on the Olympic Peninsula. And if you seek solitude and wilderness when you fish, the beaches, rivers and lakes of Olympic National Park offer settings as remote and pristine as any place in the lower 48 states.

In the years I have lived on the Olympic Peninsula, I have thought about its fisheries in many different contexts. However, I often visualize it as one of those baskets woven by the Quileute Indians, the coastal tribe that has lived at the mouth of the Quillayute River for centuries. Like the baskets, the end product is grander and more complex than the individual pieces. Indeed, I now think of the fish themselves as separate strands in a larger design, a design that includes the peninsula's elk and otters, its tide flats and trees, and backcountry peaks.

Raymond Carver, the master short story writer and poet who made the Olympic Peninsula his home, loved these waters and fish as much as anyone. In his poem "Where Water Comes Together With Other Water" he writes about the peninsula waters this way:

"...the places streams flow into rivers.
The open mouths of rivers where they
join the sea
the places where water comes together
with other water. Those places stand out
in my mind like holy places.
But those coastal rivers!
I love them the way some men love horses
or glamorous women. I have a thing
for this cold swift water.
Just looking at it makes my blood run
and my skin tingle. I could sit
and watch these rivers for hours.
Not one of them like any other..."

When I decided to write this book, it was my intention to celebrate the unique fish and fisheries of the Olympic Peninsula, not to create a "how-to" book for the area. However, since I firmly believe a knowledge of the run timing of the peninsula's fish is half the battle when approaching these waters, I can't help thinking that fishermen that read this book should have a lot less trouble getting started out here than I did. Indeed, to give readers a sense of the cyclical pulse of the peninsula's fish, I have, reluctantly and inevitably, organized it around that most hoary of all angling clichés—a seasonal framework.

Knowing where the fish lie, in my opinion, is the other half of the battle—not tackle or flies. And before you read any further, I want to say that I'm not going to reveal any secret holes. I don't think it's fair to benefit from the hard won knowledge of local fishermen for a few minutes of notoriety and a couple of bucks. Second, if I did reveal all of the best locations on Olympic rivers and lakes, I'd be beaten up—by my own friends. If you aren't good at reading water, read some books or articles, take a course, or hire a guide to tutor you. But the only real way to learn how to anticipate where fish lie, is to put in time on the water.

That's the way it works out here anyway.

The pristine seacoasts, remote mountain peaks and rain forest valleys of Olympic National Park offer fly fishermen the richest and most diverse variety of angling settings in the lower 48 states.

Natives

You would think that I would be sick of steelhead by March. After all, they have been pretty much the only game in town since Thanksgiving. That's three months. Three months of rain-swollen rivers and icy roads. Three months of figuring how to get away from the out-of-towners that descend on the Olympic Peninsula each winter when the big hatchery runs are in the Bogachiel and Elwha, Calawah and Lyre. Three months of casting heavy lines and unwieldy flies for fish that aren't even hungry, for god's sake.

So you would think that I would be sick of steelhead by March. But I'm not. You see, this is the time of year when many of the largest native steelhead return to Olympic rivers. Weighing 15, 20, 25 pounds, these fish have spent three, four or even five years at sea. They are the vigorous, leaping, nearly tireless battlers that have made the word steelhead one of the most evocative in all of angling. And as springtime unfolds, they often hold in shallow tailouts and runs and respond aggressively to a well-presented fly.

This is also a wonderful time of year to be on a steelhead stream. "...the flowers were in bloom, the birds singing, the grouse drumming, the pine squirrels chattering," is the way a springtime steelhead outing was described in Port Angeles newspaper publisher E.B. Webster's delightful 1923 book *Fishing in the Olympics*. In addition, the throngs that pursue the hatchery runs of early winter have hung up their rods by now. And although most of the small streams are closed now, the large rivers of the peninsula's remote "West End" usually remain open into April.

During early spring, the relentless winter storms are often replaced by short periods of moderate rain, followed by cool, dry weather. Consequently, the large rivers are often surprisingly low and clear in springtime. This makes it easier to work a fly line, even a dry line on occasion.

As with most things in life, you can have too much of a good thing—even dry weather on the Olympic Peninsula. Several years ago, for example, a sharp cold front drifted down from the interior of British Columbia during the first week of March. For 10 days, the rivers flowed low and clear, through panes of ice. At first, fly fishermen did well. But eventually the steelhead became that peculiar combination of torpid and spooky that cold weather fishermen know all too well. After months of wanting nothing more than a break in the North Pacific's relentless barrage of storms, fly fishermen now just as fervently were hoping for rain.

Then one evening the weatherman had good news: A big, low pressure system from the Gulf of Alaska would spin into the north coast of Washington during the night. Bringing heavy rain and warming temperatures, the storm was supposed to last for three or four days. That was just what I had been wanting to hear. I set my alarm for three o'clock. As I lay awake, I ticked off the list of rivers I could fish the next morning—the Queets, the Hoh and the Quinault in the rain forest; the Bogachiel and Calawah and Dickey of the Quillayute System. But then I thought of a run on the Sol Duc where the river breaks hard into a sandstone bank, then ripples over sunken, waist-deep shelves. I hoped I could hit it at that magic moment after the rain had quickened the river's pulse and warmed it, but before it picked up enough flow to make fly fishing difficult.

It hadn't started raining when I left my home in Port Townsend the next morning.

In fact, the stars were still shining, and I had to scrape ice from my windshield. I watched for patches of black ice as I headed west on U.S. 101. Passing through the sleeping communities of Sequim and Port Angeles, I saw the twinkling lights of Victoria on the southern tip of Vancouver Island, fifteen miles across the inky darkness of the Strait of Juan de Fuca.

I could have fished the Elwha River. One of the largest rivers on the peninsula, the Elwha flows into the strait five miles west of Port Angeles. But Elwha native steelhead are one of the most distressed stocks on the peninsula, having been confined to a five-mile stretch of supine water below a hydroelectric dam since 1912. The Sol Duc, on the other hand, has one of the longest anadromous reaches on the Olympic Peninsula, more than 50 miles. Sol Duc wild winter steelhead, not surprisingly, are one of the healthiest stocks on the Olympic Peninsula. Because of the relatively intact condition of its watershed and the absence of glaciers in its headwaters, the Sol Duc also stays in shape longer than other large Olympic rivers and cleans up much more rapidly after a storm.

In addition to practical considerations, fly fishermen have sentimental reasons to fish the Sol Duc's clear-flowing waters. The Sol Duc is where Syd Glasso created the Olympic Peninsula's steelhead fly fishing heritage in the 1950s and '60s. Glasso's legendary 18-and -3/4-pound winter steelhead, the largest fly-caught steelhead entered in *Field & Stream's* Angling Competition in 1959, was a Sol Duc fish. The Sol Duc was also Glasso's proving ground for the Sol Duc and Heron series of Spey flies. These astonishingly beautiful flies put a uniquely North American stamp on the venerable Scottish Atlantic salmon patterns and earned Glasso international acclaim as a fly tier.

I pressed on through the darkness and ice toward the rim of the continent. A few miles west of P.A., as Port Angeles is known on the peninsula, the little clots of early morning traffic all but disappeared. The only other people on the road were a few log trucks, their lights cutting yellow swatches across the frosty road, and an occasional macho-looking 4X4 towing a drift boat. I crossed the Elwha River at the bottom of the long grade, then grabbed the steering wheel purposefully.

The stretch of highway between the Elwha and Lake Sutherland known as Indian Valley lies on the north side of Baldy Ridge. During the winter and early spring, the pale southern sun never climbs above the top of the ridge. Frost coats the ground and trees all day during cold weather. It isn't uncommon to see vehicles in the ditch, some resting on their roofs.

Driving through the valley, though, I noticed that not only were the log trucks driving fast, but so were the occasional truck or passenger cars. I tested my brakes gingerly and felt the satisfying bite of tread on pavement. Then I noticed that the stars were no longer visible. The front had rolled in, as predicted. It wasn't raining yet, but the cloud cover deepened each mile I traveled west. I had my wipers on by the time I reached 10-mile-long Lake Crescent; Olympic Peninsula mist and fog can be as drenching as full-blown rain.

As I passed the road that follows the Sol Duc upstream into the Olympic National Park, I thought of my friend, 84-year-old Roy Bergstrom. Nearly half a century earlier, Roy took three heavy steelhead from the upper river, then suffered terribly trying to drag them through crusty, waist-deep snow back to his car. These days, the headwaters are closed during the winter to provide a sanctuary to spawning steelhead. I stayed on 101, paralleling the river's westward course to the sea.

It began to rain as I crossed the Snider Creek Bridge, the current upper limit of open water during the winter. Largely through the efforts of West End fly fishing guide Bob Pigott, the 10-mile stretch of river between the Snider Creek Bridge and the salmon hatchery at Sappho is now catch and release for wild steelhead during the winter, and anglers are restricted to single hook flies and artificial lures. In recent years, local citizens, the Forest Service and the Olympic Peninsula Guides Association have also operated a rearing pond at Snider Creek for fish spawned from line-caught wild Sol Duc winter steelhead.

I turned off the highway a couple of miles east of the small logging community of Forks. As I passed the shake mill next to the Smokehouse Restaurant, I smelled the sweet aroma of burning cedar and saw orange sparks spilling from the top of its burn tower. I drove past the log road that winds down to the confluence of the Bogachiel and Calawah rivers. The run I planned to fish was only a couple of miles away now.

Suddenly, I had one of those unbidden flickers of self-awareness. Here I am, I thought, driving through a pouring rain in the dark, with less than five hours of sleep, and I am happy. As a matter of fact, I realized, it was for days exactly like this that I had made the Olympic Peninsula my home. Indeed, as much as I love scrambling up to high country lakes; however much I like fishing the ragged coastline and kelp-tangled bays—and as compelling as I find skating a dry fly through the low water slicks of autumn—I have gradually come to understand that it is the Olympic Peninsula's winter steelhead that keep me here.

After all, where else can I fish for such magnificent fish this time of year? Not in Michigan, where I grew up; even in the lower peninsula, early March is a time of filthy snow and rotting ice, with the glories of the river opener a month away. Not in the Rocky Mountains; I've spent enough time dead-drifting nymphs through deep pools for logy trout and whitefish for this lifetime, thank you. And not in central Oregon, either; there are still a dozen feet of snow over the Cascade Lakes Highway, and Crane Prarie, Wickiup, Hosmer, Davis and Sparks won't turn on until late spring and early summer. Even the Florida Keys, where I lived in the late 1970s, aren't at their best

this time of year—the sailfish in the Gulfstream are tapering off, and the back-country angling won't peak until the water warms up in May.

The remote, rain-washed steelhead rivers of the West End, however, are most productive during winter and early spring. Indeed, the peninsula is one of the few places in the country where the bulk of the freshwater angling effort takes place between Thanksgiving and the opening day of baseball season. And although winter steelhead fly fishing is demanding, with many days often elapsing between hook-ups, persistent, disciplined anglers eventually land fish. Even more important, I can still find solitude and room for a backcast out here if I fish on weekdays and avoid the popular spots.

On that early March morning, I swung the car off the pavement a few miles above the confluence of the Sol Duc and Bogachiel. I splashed down a muddy logging road for several miles, then parked in a small turn-around. I was relieved when I saw there were no other vehicles, the run can accommodate two or three drift fishermen but only one fly fisherman. If someone had arrived before me, I would have turned around and gone somewhere else.

I wriggled into my waders and grabbed my eight-weight and vest. Although it was still raining, the Olympic Peninsula nighttime had begun to yield to a murky, pre-dawn gray. The trail down to the river is often a morass of mud, but it still held the freeze of the previous week and walking was easy. However, the bottle-brush boughs of the Sitka spruce drenched me in spray every time I brushed against one.

I could hear the sound of water moving over rock before I could see the river. After scrambling under a final moss-covered arm of vine maple, I emerged from the trees onto the cobble and mud of the Sol Duc's bank. The river broke against the sand outcrop directly across from me. It then flowed evenly for the 40-yard-length of the run before plaiting around an alder-covered island. In early spring, the steelhead hang in the sandy slots along the bottom of the run.

Sol Duc is a corruption of the local Indian word Sol'Il Tak, which means "sparkling water", and in the grainy half light the Sol Duc's limpid green water did indeed shimmer. From the look of the water, slapping gently on the windows of ice along its banks, I could tell that the river had already risen a few inches. That was just what I wanted. I quickly strung my floating line, then looped on a 10-foot section of high-density sink tip. I tied on a leech pattern.

I checked the bite of my fly's hook and tested my tippet knot. Then I waded into position a dozen yards above and across from a large shelf. I stripped a few coils of line and made a short across-stream cast. I fished the fly dead-drift as it passed through the slot. But instead of tossing slack and raising my rod tip to extend the drag-free float, I let the current lift the fly in a traditional wet-fly swing as it drifted past the holding water.

I'm a firm believer in the magic of first casts, but I seldom hook fish on my first cast, especially winter steelhead, which often seem to need to be coaxed into biting. So I was surprised when I felt the sharp jolt of a strike. But when the thick, black back of the fish broke the surface, I was stunned.

It's a salmon, I thought. Earlier in the week, Roy Bergstrom told me that he had taken a spring chinook from the Bark Hole on the Sol Duc. My glimpse of this fish's back reminded me of big kings I had slipped nets under on the Strait of Juan de Fuca and Admiralty Inlet. It also fought the dogged, bruising heavyweight battle of a chinook, with none of the lively grace or speedy acrobatics of a middleweight, like a steelhead.

But then it jumped. It cleared the water in one of those low-trajectory, vaulting leaps that big fish make. Even in the rainy gloom, I could see that it was a steelhead, the biggest steelhead I had ever seen. It's 25 pounds, I remember thinking. That

was five pounds larger than the biggest steelhead I had ever taken.

Before I had a chance to play the fish—before I even had a chance to visualize telling my friends about it—my line snapped. And I mean snapped. One minute, my rod was bent into a question mark and I was holding onto a tight, throbbing line, the next there was a loud pop, like the breaking of the high E string on a classical guitar.

I stood there for a minute, utterly disconsolate. After a while, though, my curiosity got the better of me. What in the world happened, I wondered? I'd just checked my knot. As it turned out, I hadn't checked the right knot. The line had pulled apart at the junction of my leader and the stiff 12-inch section of 40-pound line I used as a leader butt.

When I realized that was about the same diameter as a high E on a classical guitar, I laughed. It wasn't a very hearty laugh, however.

With its clear water, healthy run of natives and catch-and-release area, the Sol Duc is a natural for fly fishermen in March and April. But the Sol Duc's sister Quillayute System rivers—the Bogachiel, Calawah and Dickey—support robust runs of natives as well. Impressive numbers of thick-shouldered rain forest steelhead also return to the Hoh, Queets and Quinault. And after years of decline, the Chehalis River tributaries that drain the southern Olympics—the Wishkah, Wynoochee and Satsop—once again host good numbers of wild fish when the salmonberry are in bloom.

Rising on the opposite side of High Divide and Bogachiel Peak as the Sol Duc, and flowing westward over a roughly parallel course, the Bogachiel River joins the Sol Duc six miles from the ocean to form the Quillayute River. In good years as many as 4,500 natives return to the Bogachiel, ranking it among the Olympic Peninsula's greatest winter steelhead rivers. The good fly water is more spread out on the Bogachiel than the Sol Duc, however, which gives anglers with boats an advantage. The Bogachiel is also a safer river to float than the Sol Duc or Calawah, neither of which should be attempted by novice drift boat operators.

The largest tributary to the Bogachiel, the Calawah often runs very low and clear during springtime. This tends to send fishermen with boats over to rivers with more flow like the Bogachiel or Hoh. But river conditions that rankle drift fishermen and plug pullers are often perfect for fly fishermen, especially anglers willing to experiment with nymphs, no hackle flies and summer class lines and tippets. And although there is limited easy access to the mainstem Calawah (the north and south forks are usually closed in springtime), fishermen that study county and Department of Natural Resources maps and don't mind hoofing a mile or two down an abandoned logging road on a hunch, eventually find both excellent fly water and solitude.

The Dickey River empties into the Quillayute about a mile upstream of the ocean. Unlike the other major Quillayute tributaries, which usually carry the tinge of green that steelheaders refer to as color, the Dickey is tanin-stained from the leaching of cedar swamps in its headwaters. The Dickey is also much smaller than the other Quillayute rivers, with the most distant water within reach of a middling fly caster. Fed by a west, middle and north fork, the Dickey watershed sprawls over an immense area of remote lowlands and cut-over hills. Even more than the Calawah, this intimate river of log-jams and native steelhead is the realm of independent, exploring anglers.

If the Quillayute rivers—clear, with relatively stable flows and comprehensible water—are the winter steelhead rivers of the conscious mind, the ones you would construct if asked to design a system of steelhead rivers, then the Hoh, Queets and Quinault are the rivers of your dreams. Indeed, there is something undeniably mythic about the rain forest rivers. Brawling and unpredictable, these glacial torrents pos-

sess the terrible power to rip 200-foot-tall trees from the bank and carve out new channels overnight. Yet they are also places of rapt silence, where you find yourself talking in whispers as you walk through the woods on the way to the river. And rain forest steelhead are, along with the ravens and elk and ancient trees, the totems of this myth.

Sometimes, however, the rain forest steelhead seem more mythical than mythic. For fly fishermen especially, the native steelhead of the Hoh, Queets and Quinault can be frustratingly elusive. To begin with, the rain forest rivers' vastness—the seemingly featureless 100-yard-long runs and pools the size of revival tents—can be intimidating to fishermen accustomed to more clearly defined pool, tailout, riffle sequences. Because of their bedload of glacial flour, the pulverized rock that the glaciers mill from the mountains, rain forest rivers present a visibility challenge to fly fishermen even in good spring weather. During periods of heavy rain or glacier-melting warm spells, they look like wet cement.

Successful rain forest steelheaders usually wait for stretches of dry cool weather, which lock up the glaciers. They also fish big, flashy flies on quick sinking lines. Most important of all, they discipline themselves to concentrate on a few specific areas—creek mouths, for instance, or rocky sections of pocket water. Like a quail hunter picking a single bird from a covey, they ignore the big picture and focus intently on water that can be fished effectively with a fly.

As for the rivers of the Olympic's southern boundary, the largest sport-caught steelhead in Washington state for many years was a 25-pounder from the Chehalis River. By the 1980s, however, decades of poor logging practices, overfishing and pollution of the Grays Harbor estuary had resulted in a marked decline in native steelhead returns to the Chehalis and its northern tributaries. In what has become the Olympic Peninsula's outstanding example of a cooperative, long-term fisheries restoration project, local residents, logging companies like Mayr Brothers Logging, Trout Unlimited, Long Live the Kings and the Chehalis and Quinault tribes cooperated with the state to reclaim degraded habitat and to restore stocks of wild Chehalis Basin steelhead and salmon. Today, anglers have a better shot at a wild springtime steelhead on the Satsop, Wynoochee, Wishkah and Hoquiam than in any time in years.

In his classic book, *Steelhead Fly Fishing and Flies*, Trey Combs quotes an article Syd Glasso wrote for "The Creel," the newsletter of the Flyfishers of Oregon.

"I regret more and more the vanity that lets me kill one of these fish. Must I prove that I've caught something? It's ridiculous to become sentimental over a fish, and yet those desperate, all-out fights at the end of a leader do deserve something better than a final blow on the head."

Glasso was something of a visionary when he expressed those sentiments in 1970. During the intervening quarter-century, however, catch and release of native steelhead has become the prevailing ethic of Northwestern fly fishing. Indeed, many recent converts to the sport cringe at the idea of killing even hatchery steelhead.

In recent years, Olympic National Park and the Washington Department of Fish and Wildlife have also adopted much more aggressive strategies to protect native steelhead on the peninsula. For example, mandatory release of all wild winter steelhead is now in effect on the upper reaches of the Queets, Hoh and Bogachiel within the national park. The hike-in water on the Bogachiel in the park is, in addition, currently restricted to artificial lures during the winter. In an attempt to protect and restore weak native stocks, the WDFW has imposed catch-and-release regulations for all wild winter steelhead on Hood Canal tributaries, the Dungeness and the Satsop and Chehalis.

"Our number one emphasis on the Chehalis is wild fish," Region 6 fisheries biologist Bill Freymen explains. "Everything we do is driven by our desire for wild fish to reach escapement goals."

Unfortunately, the battle is far from over. As more and more Puget Sound and Columbia River winter stocks flounder, the pressure on the lower reaches of the large West End rivers has increased dramatically. This compromises the solitude that used to be a given on these rivers in the spring. Much more alarming, however, is the fact that many of these fishermen keep every steelhead they catch, hatchery fish and natives alike.

Unbelievably, the editors of the sporting press encourage this irresponsible behavior. Each spring these publications run pieces that trumpet the fact that you can still "catch and keep" on sections of the Hoh, Sol Duc and other West End rivers. The articles usually conclude with a half-hearted admonition that "you might want to release natives—unless you take that 'once-in-a-lifetime' fish." Predictably enough, the writers became positively hysterical over the decision by the Washington Fish and Wildlife Commission to impose limits on the harvest of native winter steelhead on West End rivers— even though they would still have allowed anglers to kill as many as eight wild fish a year!

Perhaps even more troubling is the fact that some Olympic Peninsula politicians have seized upon native steelhead as a vehicle to debate "county rights" and to divert attention from how land use and habitat issues effect anadromous fish stocks. A majority of the Clallam County Commissioners, for example, demanded a meeting with the Department of Fish and Wildlife after the vote of the Fish and Wildlife Commission, claiming the county should have a voice in how to manage the fish within its boundaries. And 24th District State Representative Jim Buck said he opposed the restrictions because the steelhead runs were healthy and didn't require special regulations.

Buck's announcement was far from surprising. One of his first acts after taking office in 1995 was to ask statistician Robert Crittenden to draft fisheries legislation for him. The author of the self-published screed, "Salmon at Risk," Crittenden maintains that control of anadromous fish should be handed over to the counties, where they will be managed for "subsistence fishing and commercial fishing by local user-owned small businesses." According to Crittenden, "subsistence fishing" is sport fishing "where the catch is consumed." He has also written that catch-and-release would only be allowed "at locations and times where they aren't unduly in competition with subsistence or local small business commercial fishing."

That this is the same sort of myopic, self-indulgent nonsense that has helped to destroy native fish runs throughout the Northwest goes without saying. Indeed, many of the "once-in-a-lifetime" fish that end up on the walls of family rooms—and in people's stomachs—die before they have passed on their irreplaceable genetic legacy even one time.

"Most of the Hoh's biggest steelhead are males on their initial spawning run," explains Jim Jorgensen, Hoh Tribe fisheries biologist. "A lot of people think that the really big fish are repeat spawners. But actually each time a steelhead returns to a river and spawns it loses weight. It has to make that weight up out at sea. On the other hand, fish that stay out to sea longer than usual— for four, maybe even five years—continue to grow. Consequently, the biggest steelhead are usually first-time spawners."

Biologists and fishing guides approach steelhead from widely different perspectives, and they don't always agree on how the fish should be managed. But Bob Pigott, the fly fishing guide that wrote and lobbied for the "wild steelhead release" and "no bait" regulations on the upper Sol Duc, is also a passionate advocate for native steelhead.

"We can't spare a single wild fish on these rivers," Bob says emphatically. "Partial closures, when they close the upper part of a river, sound good. But all that really does is put a lot of pressure on the downstream spawners. And hatcheries can be a good idea if the run is gone. But sport fishermen and tribal fishing always knock down wild fish when a river has a hatchery run.

"We have so much water out here," Bob continues. "And we have plenty of excellent habitat left. The obvious answer is mandatory wild release. If we went to that for five years, we would have more steelhead than you can shake a stick at. We've just got to stop killing these fish."

Chapter 2

The Hoko

Dead-drifting an egg pattern on a floating line requires concentration, probably more concentration than any other steelhead fly fishing technique. But my mind was about as far from the Hoko River's tea-colored water as it could be when the fish hit. In fact, my thoughts had carried me back to the mid-nineteenth century and to James Swan, one of the first white men to see the remote northwest corner of the Olympic Peninsula that the Hoko flows through.

Fortunately, the steelhead hooked itself. A firecracker of a fish, it tailwalked across the pool, then sliced downstream. On a big river with plenty of room, I would have let it run, let the rod and weight of the line wear it down a bit. But the upper Hoko is a tangle of snags and sweepers and brushy cutbanks, so I chased it. At one point, I had to pass my rod under a fir sweeper. I also fell down twice and ripped a hole in my favorite wool shirt. But the fish was hooked solidly, and I managed to keep slack out of the line. Ten minutes later and 100 yards downstream, I slipped the barbless hook from the jaw of a chunky six-pounder. I released it.

I sat down on a spongy cedar snag and found the sandwich in my vest. I was still excited and played back the battle in my mind. I remembered its charcoal back, the salmonberry blossom splash on its gill plates. But by the time I finished eating, I had begun to think about Swan again.

A well-bred Bostonian, James Gilchrist Swan sailed around Cape Horn to San Francisco in 1850. After side trips to the gold fields and Hawaii, Swan secured work with a waterfront shipping supply company. San Francisco was bustling, raw and colorful during the Gold Rush, and Swan reveled in its freedoms. But two years later, perhaps driven by the same sense of adventure that had pulled him from Boston, he accepted an offer to manage an oyster harvesting operation on Shoalwater Bay in Washington Territory.

During the mid-1850s, Shoalwater Bay was for all practical purposes wilderness. Yet for someone who had spent his entire life in cities, Swan adapted quickly to the tidal and seasonal rhythms of life on the bay. He made friends with the local Chinook and Chehalis Indians. He developed a taste for the local cuisine, the ducks and salmon, elk and shellfish. He filed a land claim and helped build a cabin.

Swan fell back on the technique of an Eastern gentleman the first time he approached a nearby stream with a fishing rod. "I tried my hand with flies," he wrote in his 1857 book *The Northwest Coast*, "but they were of no account on these uncivilized fish."

Two years later, having succumbed completely to the enchantments of the Pacific Northwest, Swan moved to Neah Bay on the northwest tip of the Olympic Peninsula. For the next forty years, Swan divided his time between the Makah Indian village at Neah Bay and the Victorian seaport of Port Townsend. During that time, he developed a national reputation as an authority on Northwestern Indians and contributed artifacts and writings to the Smithsonian Institution. He also published books, taught school and served as a judge. But although the Hoko and other streams near Neah Bay teemed with steelhead, salmon and trout, he apparently never cast a fly again.

Other early Olympic Peninsula anglers enjoyed considerable success with flies, however. Homesteaders along lowland creeks and lakes regularly took cutthroat on cast and trolled flies. The expeditions that explored the interior of the Olympic Mountains in the 1890s reported excellent backcountry river fishing. And in *Fishing in the Olympics*, E.B. Webster described early 20th century fishing on the Elwha River this way: "A four or five pound rainbow is just a common eating fish, the same as a nine or ten pound salmon. You catch them on a brown hackle, a coachman or professor, or a belle."

When it came to Olympic Peninsula winter steelhead, however, Swan's observation carried the weight of received wisdom for more than a century. Long after the first fly-caught winter steelhead was taken from California's Eel River in the 1890s—and decades after the practice climbed the rungs of coastal rivers all the way to the Skagit and Campbell—the overwhelming majority of Olympic Peninsula anglers dismissed winter steelhead fly fishing out of hand. "Eggs will get you a fish," they never tired of saying. "And sand shrimp and plugs. And spoons sometimes. But flies? No way." Olympic rivers, it was believed, were simply too fast, too steep and too often roiled by rain for cold weather fly fishing.

Of course, this was not true. Syd Glasso, Dick Wentworth and a handful of anglers proved that on many occasions during the 1950s and 60s. But the tavern stool experts' assessment of Olympic Peninsula rivers was correct in one sense: They are fast, ferrying the heaviest rainfall in the lower 48 states to sea over watercourses that are typically less than 40 miles long. They are steep, losing as much as 5,000 feet of elevation in as little as 25 river-miles. And they are often unfishable for days at a time during the winter.

When you factor in an essentially dour fish like a winter steelhead and the unwieldy (and relatively ineffective) tackle of the era, Olympic Peninsula winter steelhead fly fishing became a rather daunting proposition. Not surprisingly, only a handful of anglers possessed the resolve and the skill to take these fish on the fly. For the first three-quarters of this century, winter fly fish-

ermen were so rare on Olympic rivers as to be essentially invisible.

All that began to change, however, when the fishing tackle industry introduced lightweight, fast-action graphite rods and sink tip lines in the 1970s. Gradually at first, then at a steadily increasing pace, Olympic Peninsula anglers began to exchange drift and spinning rods for fly rods. Most of the new fly fishermen stuck to warm weather fly fishing initially, concentrating on sea-run cutthroat, the resident trout of the Elwha and summer steelhead on the Quillayute and Rain Forest rivers. But by the time local anglers formed a chapter of the Federation of Fly Fishers in the early 1980s, a significant number of fishermen had begun to pursue winter steelhead with the fly.

The late James Garrett was the obvious choice to lead the group. An immensely gifted fly tier and fisherman, Garrett had developed dozens of patterns for Olympic fish and rivers. He also single-handedly introduced an entire new generation of fishermen to fly tying at courses he taught at the local community college and, later, at the Quality Fly Fishing Shop in Port Angeles.

"The club used to meet in the basement of his house at the Dungeness salmon hatchery," recalls J.D. Love, a long-time peninsula fly fishing guide and charter member of the group.

As in most such organizations, one of its first objectives was to try to secure a section of fly-only water.

"Originally, we wanted the upper Sol Duc or a portion of the Hoh," J.D. says, "but the Washington Department of Game told us they wouldn't close any section of a river that was already open. They told us to find a section of a river that was already closed. They were against 'elitist' regulations."

Eventually, the group settled for November through March "fly-fishing-only" catch-and-release regulations on an eight-mile stretch of the upper Hoko River. On the surface, the Hoko was a curious choice to become the Northwest's first fly-only water for winter steelhead. A small, brushy, cedar-stained tributary to the western Strait of Juan de Fuca, the Hoko is a far remove, both physically and atmospherically, from the large coastal rivers where Glasso and Garrett established the Olympic Peninsula's fly fishing traditions. In addition, the fly water is located on private timberlands at the end of a labyrinth of logging roads, which can be gated at any time.

"In my opinion, it was not an ideal place for fly-only water," J.D. observes, reflecting the views of most long-time peninsula fly anglers.

Still, the river had its attributes—most notably, a run of native winter steelhead that was in good shape, especially good shape compared to the runs on most small and medium-sized rivers in western Washington. The Makah tribal enhancement program was also based entirely on native Hoko broodstock rather than the early-returning Chambers Creek stock that was the standard on other Olympic Peninsula rivers at the time. In addition, the Hoko is too small for drift boats, and its access problems and remoteness discourage all but the most intrepid anglers.

As on all small steelhead waters, fly fishermen pay as close attention to the weather on the Hoko as fishermen on the Ausable, Henry's Fork and Deschutes do to insect hatches. The best time to hit the river is usually a few days after a substantial freshet. That gives fresh, active fish a chance to swim into the upper river. On the other hand, prolonged storms or dry weather tend to produce poor fishing, because the steelhead either blast into the headwaters or sulk in the lower river.

A fly fished dead-drift often produces better on small water than a fly on a swing. "I usually fish a Glo Bug on the Hoko," J.D.

explains. "I use a single-handed rod, a leader the length of the rod and a floating line."

The Hoko, of course, will never supplant the coastal rivers in the minds and hearts of fly fishermen that love the Olympic Peninsula. For visiting anglers, especially, the Sol Duc and Calawah, the Bogachiel and Hoh are the big draws during the winter steelhead season. But the handful of anglers that have taken the time to learn the Hoko's tight pools and shallow tailouts now consider it an integral part of springtime steelheading. They like its solitude, the fact that almost no one goes to the bother of finding the fly water. Furthermore, the catch-and-release regulations and the Hoko's healthy run allow the river to remain open through March, a month longer than other small West End rivers.

"We've been getting twice the number of spawners we need for escapement," Washington Department of Fish and Wildlife Region 6 biologist Bill Freyman explained to me a few years after the fly-only regulations went into effect.

Finally, anglers with a sense of history savor the irony that the Hoko became the first winter steelhead fly water in Washington. The Olympic Peninsula, after all, was the last place on the North Pacific coast where fly rods became anything more than curiosities. Moreover, 150 years after Swan dismissed coastal fish as too uncivilized for flies, the only fly-only water on the peninsula is on a river Swan sailed past every time he traveled between Neah Bay and Port Townsend. Swan had a writer's sensibility and I'm sure he'd get a kick out of this. I am also certain that if he were around today he would pick up a graphite rod and sink tip and roam the upper Hoko when the skunk cabbage are in bloom.

Chapter 3

Olympic
Littoral

I guess I have John Shewey to thank for sparking my interest in fly fishing the rugged Pacific coastline. Or perhaps I should put that another way: Maybe I have John Shewey to blame for the lack of healthful, high-protein fish in my diet since I began dragging a fly rod down to the Olympic Peninsula beaches.

You see, until about 10 years ago, I was perfectly happy to fish for the redtail surfperch and greenling, the black rockfish and flounder off the Olympic coast the same way as everyone else does out here—with a 10-foot surf rod and a spinning reel big enough to winch an elk quarter out of a ravine. The fact that I was a little overgunned for one-pound surfperch and two-pound rockfish with this outfit hadn't escaped me. When I hitchhiked back east to see the Atlantic Ocean in 1969, I saw fishermen land 20-pound striped bass and big bluefish off the tip of Cape Cod on similar tackle. Nevertheless, just about everyone out here used these big rigs for surf fishing, and they caught fish. So I followed suit. I caught fish, too.

Then I began to read John Shewey's articles in *Salmon Trout Steelheader* and *Flyfishing* magazines describing his exploits for rockfish with a fly. By that time, I had already begun to fish for black rockfish from the Neah Bay jetty with flies, and had made a few hapless attempts along the log booms in Port Angeles harbor. But Shewey sometimes talked about actually scrambling around out there at the edge of the rockfish's habitat. That intrigued me.

To say that I didn't have a lot of success in this endeavor early on is sort of like saying a ratfish is not an especially attractive creature. Looking back on it, I think it took me longer to get my first fish from the rocks than it took me to take my first steelhead on

a fly. But I was determined. I cut my fingers and knees on the barnacle- and mussel-encrusted rocks along Highway 112 between Sekiu and Neah Bay. I slipped on boulders covered with rock weed near Rialto Beach. And a heavy wave knocked me off the edge of the drop-off at Ruby Beach, then slammed me—drenched, gasping and terrified—back onto the cobble beach.

Actually, there are easier ways to catch Olympic Peninsula bottomfish on the fly. Anglers in small power boats take a variety of inshore rockfish and greenling from the immense mats of kelp between Neah Bay and Pillar Point. During late spring, these fishermen even tempt black rockfish on white surface flies on occasion. A few nocturnal fly fishermen use Coleman lanterns to draw schools of forage fish and crustaceans to jetties and piers, then dredge the depths for the fish drawn to the bait. And perhaps the Olympic Peninsula's most underexploited fishery is for the flatfish—the starry flounder, sand dabs and sand sole—of the shallow bays and river deltas along the western shore of Admiralty Inlet and Hood Canal.

But I am hopelessly under the thrall of the Olympic Peninsula's wilderness seacoast. I have always been in love with the ocean, with both the idea of it (the notion that "Hey, the next piece of land that way is Korea.") and with its reality, its smell and its taste and sound. Olympic National Park's 57-mile-long "coastal strip" is the most pristine sea coast in the lower 48 states. Within the Coastal Strip, moreover, the fog-shrouded bays, sandy beaches and offshore seastacks of the North Wilderness Coast (21 miles) and the South Wilderness Coast (18 miles) are only accessible by road in three places! For me, the chance to hoist a pack and wander for days along a virtually undisturbed seacoast is irresistible.

But that first rockfish came hard, real hard. On some trips, I spent nearly all of my time peeling kelp off my fly. Other times, the relentless coastal breeze seemed determined to pierce my ear with my keel fly. And on still other occasions, pounding surf made wading impossible. I became discouraged several times and avoided the coast for months. But a new John Shewey article would always rekindle my enthusiasm, and I would begin to fuss with tide tables and topo maps again.

Finally, after a fruitless day of early spring trout fishing on a West End lake, I stopped by the old Bear Creek Tavern near Sappho. There was only one other person in the place, besides the bar maid, an old-timer who had spent more than 50 years hunting and fishing on the West End. He was hunched over and thin but still had the big hands and knotted forearms of someone who spent his life working in the woods. We talked about elk and cougar hunting. He told me how he once caught enough summer chinook from the Sol Duc in one week to can for the entire winter.

"Too damned many people around here now," he said, slamming his can of Budweiser down on the wooden bar for emphasis. "That's the problem. Too god-damned many people."

I nodded. "How far up the Sol Duc did the chinook go in those days?"

He was lost in memories and beer, however, and didn't respond to my question.

"I used to catch all the cod and sea bass I wanted on hand lines, too," he said. "I had this place out there on the coast. I could sit on the rocks and just see them fish swimming around like they was in a fish bowl."

I took a shallow pull on my beer. "The fish aren't there any more?"

"I don't know," he said. "I ain't been up there since that cable smashed my knee."

"Where was it?" I asked casually.

He described a small rocky cove on the North Coastal Strip. I had hiked by it several times while backpacking but had never fished it.

"You've got to be there when the tide is just right," he said. "If it's below five feet, you ain't got enough water. But if it's over eight feet you got too damn much."

The first thing I did when I got back to camp was find my tide book. Flipping to the tables for April, I discovered that the afternoon high tide the next day was 6.7 feet, which was perfect. Even better, high slack was at 8 p.m. That meant that the best time to fish would occur just as twilight settled over the coast and the daytime breeze began to fade. Moreover, the surf is usually safer for beach fishermen in April than during the storm-driven months of winter, and there is less kelp than during the height of the summer. Best of all, the highest concentrations of bottomfish of the year are present along the Olympic littoral in springtime.

My fly fishing resolve collapsed briefly the next day in the parking lot at the Ozette Ranger Station. For a few moments, I had a tortured interior dialogue over whether I should bring the surf rod and fly rod or just the fly rod. Then, remembering that I had only begun to take steelhead consistently on flies after I quit carrying a drift rod, I locked the big rod in the trunk. I hitched the old green Kelty pack up onto my shoulders and began the three-mile hike to Cape Alava, the westernmost point in the lower 48 states.

I could hear the cadence of the surf before I could see it. Then, after topping a final rise, I saw the bright springtime blue of the ocean through the boughs of Sitka spruce. The surf had already reclaimed more than half of the beach from the late morning low tide, but there were still acres and acres of exposed gray rocks and tide pools. A rich, rank low tide smell rose up to me as I walked down the steep trail to the beach.

Throughout the afternoon, I scrambled over drift logs, crossed slippery cobble beaches and rock-hopped over several creek mouths. It was a weekday and I only ran into two other hikers all day. As I hiked, I thought of Roy Bergstrom's Scandinavian immigrant father, Emil, who homesteaded Cape Alava near the turn of the century. I thought back even farther, to the whale-hunting Makah Indians who thrived along these beaches for thousands of years before white men arrived in North America.

With cliffs looming above me and wind-chiseled sea-stacks and islets stretching as far as I could see to the north and south, it was impossible not to also think back even more—to the creation of the Olympic Peninsula some 50 million years ago.

Often described as "a gift from the sea," the peninsula was assembled from rock formed beneath the Pacific Ocean. The relatively soft sedimentary rock that comprises the majority of the Olympic land mass was created when sand, silt and mud that washed off the continent compressed into immense bands of sandstone and shale. Molten lava also flowed up from vents and fissures in the ocean floor during this time, accumulating into towering underwater mountains called seamounts.

Between 12 and 30 million years ago, in one of the periodic cataclysms associated with "continental drift" or "plate tectonics," the eastern edge of the oceanic plate slid under the western rim of the continent. As a result of this monumental collision, a large section of the nearshore ocean bottom was sheared up onto the continental plate. This dome-shaped mass of sandstone, shale and volcanic basalt was the ancestor of the Olympic Peninsula.

Moisture-laden clouds from the Pacific Ocean immediately began to drop rain and snow on the Olympic massif. This created rivers. The rivers, which flowed off the dome in a radial pattern, carved valleys. Alpine glaciers formed when more snow fell than could melt the following summer. They rasped and gouged the high country. Approximately two million years ago, continental glaciers crept down from Canada. These towering sheets of ice reshaped the lowlands and dug the channels of the Strait of Juan de Fuca, Puget Sound and Hood Canal.

When the ice sheets finally retreated 12,000 years ago, the peninsula stood more or less in its present incarnation—an isolated 60-by-40-mile block of rock, bound on three sides by tidewater, with the highest peaks on the Pacific Coast rising above steep-walled river valleys.

Walking along the Olympics' western littoral on that April afternoon, I had little trouble imagining the monumental forces that shaped this landscape. Indeed, the Coastal Strip's ragged headlands and fog-shrouded beaches still have a raw, almost primordial feel to them. And although the geological and glacial convulsions have at least temporarily subsided, wind and rain and tide continue to sculpt the coastline.

The tide had crept up to the edge of the driftwood by the time I made camp in the trees above the old man's "fish bowl." There was almost no surf and the little cove rocked gently like a bowl of fruit jello. The sun was only three fingers above the horizon and, as I had hoped, the wind had died down almost completely. On a high tide at dusk, it was a very fishy looking place.

I quickly strung the old, fiberglass 8-weight I used for saltwater and clambered along a spine of large boulders to edge of the deep water. The other times I hiked this section of beach, I had passed it at low tide and walked through the area now covered by water. Now, I was perched on a rock three feet above the water, looking down into the "fish bowl."

It was just as he described it—vaguely circular, about the size of a boxing ring, with mussel-covered rock walls on three sides. The ocean sluiced through a small opening on the seaward edge. All around the pool, a floating mat of kelp made fly fishing impossible. But within the bowl, the water was clear, so clear I could see broken shell and anemones on the bottom.

I tied a number 6 black Keel Bugger to my short level leader. I stripped a couple of coils of my high density 10-foot sink tip. At such close quarters, an actual fly cast wasn't necessary, so I flipped a few feet of line behind me and lobbed it toward the far side of the pool. I waited a few moments, then twitched the fly slowly back toward me.

To be perfectly honest, I was so accustomed to not catching anything surf fishing I was startled when the fish hit. But I struck back instinctively, setting the hook. Then, as I regained slack and put some pressure on the fish, it zig-zagged around the bowl. It stayed deep, putting a healthy bend in my rod.

When I hooked fish on my blunderbuss surf rig, I pretty much just cranked them in to shore. On the fly rod, though, the fish put up a real battle. I remember thinking it fought like the mangrove snappers I caught when I lived in the Florida Keys. As was the case with the snappers, the black rockfish turned out to be much smaller than I imagined. It was no more than 14 inches, if that.

But I wasn't disappointed. Indeed, taking a rockfish from shore was terrific, just as I had always imagined. It was a beautiful fish, too, with that basic freshwater bass profile but a dusky charcoal color, mottled with gray. It was also more formidable looking than a freshwater bass, armored with spines and sharp fins and teeth. I slipped the hook from its mouth and released it.

As the light faded, I caught two more rockfish and a beautiful blue kelp greenling. A thin band of clouds drifted down the coast from the north. Streamers of rhinoceros auklets and tufted puffins returned to their offshore breeding grounds. I scrambled back to camp just before it was too dark to see.

I lit a match under the fire I had laid out earlier. Holding a flashlight in my mouth, I cleaned the smallish rockfish I had kept. I wiped its body cavity with olive oil, stuffed it with roughly-chopped onion, tomato, garlic and oregano, and wrapped it in aluminum foil. Then as the fire burned down to a small bed of coals, I put on a small pot of water for the Asian noodles I habitually eat when I backpack.

It was completely dark now. I placed the fish on the coals, adding a few more pieces of driftwood on top of the aluminum foil. The waves lapped at the rocky shoreline. A soft night breeze rustled the spruce boughs above me. I could see the orange flicker of another camper's fire a quarter mile up the beach.

I rooted around in my pack and found the two "airline-size" bottles of brandy in my pack. I poured them into my enameled tin cup and settled back against a bleached drift log. I took a sip of brandy and sighed.

Thanks, John, I remember thinking.

Chapter 4

Spey Flies

I t's hard to imagine a better setting for a wildlife artist's studio than the rain forest cabin where Jack Datisman turns out his paintings and drawings. Perched on a glacially-carved terrace a short distance from the Hoh River, behind the gates of a working cattle ranch, Datisman's studio offers both privacy and expansive views in several directions—not a common occurrence in the rain forest. During the winter, herds of Roosevelt elk often bed down in the pasture below the cabin. In summer, the steelhead and chinook drifts on the Hoh are only a few minutes away. The studio even carries history, as it was the retirement cabin of Minnie Peterson, a well-known Hoh Valley pioneer who packed hunters and fishermen into the Olympics during the early years of the century.

In recent years, the canvasses and watercolors that Datisman has produced in the cabin have earned him a place among the most respected wildlife artists in the Northwest. His painting *Hoh River Chinook* was selected for the Washington State Salmon Stamp in 1990. In 1994, he won Idaho Steelhead and Salmon Unlimited print of the year and the Idaho Muzzleloader permit stamp competitions. The following year the Association of Northwest Steelheaders chose his painting *Spring Chinook—Hoh* as its 1995 art print and stamp. Another measure of Jack's emerging reputation is the fact that all of his paintings now have a buyer before he paints, and there is a waiting list.

However, I hadn't come to talk about Jack's art the late spring day that I bounced up the two-track to his cabin. No, that day we had arranged to talk about Spey flies, the distinctive long-hackled patterns that Atlantic salmon fishermen developed on Scotland's Spey River Valley during the nineteenth century and that Forks-area fly-tying

pioneer Syd Glasso revived and extended to new heights during the 1950s and 1960s. Widely acknowledged as the most elegantly beautiful flies in steelhead fishing, Glasso's Sol Duc and Heron series' have proven as effective on Pacific fish as their more somber inspirations are on Atlantic salmonids. Glasso's Sol Duc accounted for the 18-3/4-pounder that was the largest fly-caught steelhead in the nation in 1959.

In the decade since Syd Glasso passed away, Spey flies have become fashionable among West Coast fly fishermen. Scores of Glasso-inspired patterns have been created, and they are fished from California to Alaska. Most Olympic Peninsula fly fishermen, however, feel affectionately proprietary about Spey flies, believing that the misty coastal rivers of the West End remain the spiritual center of the North American Spey fly. Glasso proteges like Dick Wentworth, after all, still have close ties to Olympic rivers. And it isn't uncommon to run into anglers who can regale you with Glasso stories. Many local tiers labor mightily to create replicas of Glasso patterns, then fish them enthusiastically. Jack Datisman ties some of the best.

As I said, I hadn't planned to talk about Jack's art on this visit. But it was impossible to ignore the expanse of canvas that occupied nearly the entire front room. Done in the blues and grays of a winter stream, it portrayed a steelhead about to hit a sunken fly. It wasn't completed, but it was clear that it would be a very impressive painting.

"It was commissioned by the Thrifty Mart in Forks," Jack explained, as he wiped paint off his hands.

"Wow."

"They've also commissioned an elk painting."

After the requisite complaining about

how our respective careers were keeping us from the earthly inspiration of our labors, we moved over to the small side room where Jack ties his flies. It had the familiar yet intoxicating olfactory pleasures of feather and fur, the visual delights of tinsel and floss, dyed hackles and rainbows of thread. Seeing the neatly organized materials and the well-tended tools, however, pricked me with shame at the thought of the chaotic squalor of my workplace.

As Jack assembled his materials, we talked about the Glasso patterns as fishing tools. I mentioned that most of my experience with Spey flies was during low flows in late winter and early spring. Jack, on the other hand, said he liked to fish them during autumn.

"In October after a storm, the fish out here become really active sometimes," he explained. "When the conditions are right, you can fish these flies on a greased line. That can be a lot of fun."

We had decided Jack would tie the Sol Duc Spey, one of Glasso's most beautiful inventions. It is also an instructive pattern in that its silhouette and flowing hackle are faithful to the classic Scottish flies like the Black Horse and Lady Caroline. Yet its bright yellow hackle, hot orange wings and ribs are as uniquely Northwestern as a neon Rainier beer sign in a tavern window on a rainy night.

"I became interested in Spey flies when I investigated Atlantic salmon flies for my painting," Jack said. "I had to know what went into the flies, and some of the books mentioned Spey flies. I discovered the flies weren't as fancy as Atlantic salmon flies. They were more flowing. They had a big, wide, lively-looking profile, but they got deeper than bulky patterns that try to float."

After moving to Forks from Montana, Jack picked up some of the subtleties of tying Glasso patterns from talking to Dick Wentworth, one of Glasso's most accomplished proteges. Wentworth created the Mr. Glasso pattern that is featured in Jack's painting for the Thrifty Mart, as well as the Quillayute, another Spey pattern.

"Wentworth told me that they rarely used hooks bigger than 1s," Jack recalled, as he prepared his hook.

Then we talked briefly about Deke Meyers' excellent book, *Advanced Fly Fishing for Steelhead*, which chronicles the evolution of the Spey fly in Scotland and North America. According to Meyer, anonymous Scottish ghillies crafted the first Spey flies with heron wings, the saddle hackles from Spey cocks (a large localized breed of capon that died out in the 1940s), and suggestive traces of floss, wool and tinsel. It was the heron hackle, perhaps more than anything, that gave the Spey fly the weepy, hooded look that distinguishes it from the flatter strip-wing flies of the neighboring Dee Valley and from full-dress Atlantic salmon patterns.

When Glasso created the first Spey flies for steelhead, he also used heron in a number of patterns, including the Sol Duc Spey. By the time the phenomenal beauty of his patterns had spread across the Olympic Mountains to the mainland, however, herons had became a protected species. To recreate their characteristic profile, tiers began to search for substitute materials.

"Blue-eared pheasant is the most popular substitute for heron," Jack said. "But it is very expensive and hard to get. I use Schlappen for the webby, long yellow hackle. But Wentworth has told me that we'll never again find the quality of hackles he and Glasso had."

Jack's hands moved with practiced grace as he applied the fluorescent orange floss and hot orange seal of the body. It was hard to listen, watch and make notes at the same time, especially since Jack had an interesting historical anecdote or tying tip at each step of the tying process.

"I understand that instead of using a dubbing loop, Glasso would slip the floss," he said.

"This will make it sparkle," he explained, as he picked out the seal fur.

"The idea is to create a large profile without much volume.

"Apparently Glasso tried a couple of different ways of ribbing," Jack observed. "They originally counterwrapped oval tinsel, but he supposedly didn't like that. Glasso sometimes used flat tinsel and flat and oval tinsel. The idea of the oval tinsel was to protect the feathers."

Still thinking of tinsel, he added: "There has been discussion as to whether there should be four or five wraps of tinsel. In traditional salmon patterns there are five, but most steelhead flies use four."

Next, he wound the hackle in tight against the back edge of the tinsel, pulling it back as he did it. "I kind of like to end up on the side of the eye that has the taper," he said.

The fly had begun to take on the profile that both Atlantic and Pacific fishermen have suggested resembles a shrimp or prawn.

"It's traditional to double in the throat, but I think sometimes Glasso just stripped it and used half," he remarked, as he deftly maneuvered the dyed pheasant feather. "They are fine and double easily compared to other feathers."

He paused for a moment. "I like to have a lot of room for the head, so I tie quite a ways back from the eye. That way, I can riffle hitch it if I want. Also, it is characteristic of a Spey fly to have a very small head. It should be strong but small."

Now it was time to tie in the wings. "For Spey flies, you want to find one with a fairly pronounced curve because you want the wing to ride just above the hook," he said. "It's hard to find two pairs that match."

All that was left was a whip finish and varnish.

"This is a fairly simple fly to tie compared to traditional Speys and salmon flies," Jack said.

For someone like me, who plateaued at the Gold Ribbed Hare's Ear and Woolly Bugger level of fly tying years ago, it had been an exhilarating experience, nonetheless. Indeed, I wanted to stay longer, to gather more lore and information. But I also knew what it felt like to be working on a deadline.

"Here," Jack said, handing me the fly.

Now many months later, Jack's fly rests on my writing desk. I fished with it once and took a nice cutthroat on the greased line. But I worried that I would lose it and I took it out of my vest.

Not long after that, I had a conversation with J.D. Love. I mentioned my visit with Jack, whom J.D. had worked with on a stream survey before he became a full-time guide. J.D. said that he didn't use Spey flies much with clients, preferring a more durable pattern. But he said he fished them personally quite a bit. He told me that he avoided heavy water with Spey flies and concentrated, instead, on pools and "glassy" water during late winter and spring. Like Jack, he also fished them again during the low water of autumn.

"I ran into Syd Glasso on the Calawah once," he said. "He gave me three of his flies."

"Do you still have them?"

"No," he said, with a hitch of regret in his voice. "I donated them to the trees."

Jack's fly is staying on my desk.

Chapter 5

When the
Rhodies are in Bloom

When I was a kid, all I had to do to go trout fishing was cross the county road in front of my house, walk across a big rolling pasture that skirted a marshy creek bottom, and then scramble up a steep railroad embankment. There, on the far side of the railroad tracks, a network of ponds and small lakes sprawled across a pine-fringed basin. Most of the ponds contained largemouth bass, bluegill, and sunfish, which were exciting fish. But two of the smaller ponds held trout. And by the time I was 10, I had discovered Ray Bergman's *Trout* in the Mitchell Public Library. I knew that trout were special.

So each spring after the trout season opened I became as much of a fixture along the ponds' banks as the great blue herons and mink that lived there. And since the larger pond was "fly-fishing-only" even back then, I began collecting flies. I didn't have a fly rod, but I had read in *Field & Stream* about fishing flies behind a bobber on spin gear. I bought the flies with money I made raking algae at Reed's Trout Farm and selling red worms I raised and catalpa worms that I picked off a tree in my Aunt Dorothy's yard. I mostly bought the flies I had seen in the luscious color plates in *Trout*. Like every other kid in Christendom, my favorite fly was the Royal Coachman. But I also had Black Gnats and Iron Blue Duns, McGintys and Parmachene Belles.

That was more than 30 years ago. In recent years, however, I have come to realize that a number of the patterns I repeat in my fishing and the assumptions I carry with me about fishing in general took root during those early outings on the trout ponds. For instance, I still think that trout in lakes are special. Indeed, I spend a couple of days fishing for trout in late April each year, even though it is also the last week of steelhead

fishing on the Quillayute rivers until June.

Another assumption about fishing that I developed early on is that it takes place near home. I realize that I was lucky growing up so close to good fishing water and that even back in the 1950s most people grew up in suburbs or cities. But as an adult, I have made conscious choices to live in places where I could fish close to home—rural Michigan, the Florida Keys, the Rocky Mountains, Central Oregon. I have also expanded my notion of what is close to home as I have grown older. I consider the Hoh one of my "home waters," for example, even though it is more than two hours from my house. But I'm definitely not one of those fishermen—a majority of fly fishermen, it sometimes seems—that equate fishing with travel, for whom a fishing trip involves airline tickets, reservations at a resort or lodge, and guides.

From my earliest days as a sportsman, I have always viewed fishing and hunting as basically a form of food gathering—stylized, intentionally-handicapped food gathering, perhaps, but food gathering nevertheless. Don't get me wrong, I am a fanatic about releasing native steelhead, sea-run cutthroat and wild salmon, and I would never hunt for a species whose population was depressed. But when I was a kid, a mess of bluegills, a brace of pheasants or a platter of venison chops were thought of as food, not as membership badges in some sort of elite fraternity or as proof of manhood. I still feel that way today. And when the pink splashes of rhododendron appear along the lake shores in late spring, I always think about eating trout.

Fortunately, it is easy for me to indulge both my affection and my appetite for trout close to home. You see, while the West End is the center of river fishing on the peninsula, the East Side, from Port Townsend down to Shelton, is where you find the greatest concentration of small trout lakes. Most of these low elevation, timber-bound stillwaters were originally cutthroat trout lakes. Unfortunately, unrestricted logging and agriculture obliterated nearly all of the natives' tributary spawning grounds decades ago. Today, hatchery rainbow and a handful of self-sustaining brook trout populations provide the bulk of the fishery on most East Side lakes. A small number of these non-indigenous trout grow into two- to five-pound "holdover" fish.

Of all the East Side lakes, my favorite is Gibbs Lake, a small, murky Douglas fir and cedar-bound lake a few miles south of Port Townsend. But before you add Gibbs Lake to your next trip to the peninsula, you should know that it doesn't turn out either very many or very large trout. In fact, you are much more likely to catch a small bass in Gibbs than you are a trout.

Actually, the reasons I like Gibbs Lake don't have much to do with fishing. In the first place, the physical setting of the lake—its forested shoreline, the smokey-blue hills in the distance and the one small house with its homey boat dock—reminds me of the lakes I fished as a boy. I also like the fact that it doesn't have a launch, which discourages fishermen who own boats too heavy to wrestle the 30 yards from the road down to the water. There is a lot of wildlife around the lake, too, especially in spring, when you can often see a late-departing loon and an early-arriving osprey on the same day.

But there are trout in the lake, hatchery rainbows and a few, a very few, wild cutthroat. The cutthroat are sea-runs that have swum from saltwater up Chimacum Creek to Naylors Creek, then into the lake. As on most Olympic Peninsula lowland lakes, however, legal-sized stocked rainbow trout are the main attraction on Gibbs Lake. This is especially true in late spring, when the newly-planted fish have begun to feed on insects. I have seen 14- or 15-inch holdover

trout smacking chironomid emergers, however, and people I trust have told me about 20-plus-inch fish. But I had never connected with a big fish until last year.

It was early May, but you couldn't tell it by the temperature, which climbed into the 80s each day by noon. The mornings were nice, though, soft and cool, with a sweet little breeze out the southwest. On my first day off, I wrestled my fiberglass 12-foot rowboat up into the back of my pickup and drove out to the lake. I parked by the swimming beach and dragged the boat and my gear down to the bank.

Before I mention the midges that boiled off the lake surface that morning or the mayfly hatch that came off as the first rays of sunlight hit the water, I should add that I learned another thing fishing those ponds years ago: Wet flies take trout.

In recent decades, of course, wet flies have been eclipsed by more anatomically-correct, species-based dry flies and nymphs. Wet flies have so thoroughly fallen from favor, in fact, it is now nearly impossible to find one in the vest of anyone that has been fly fishing for less than 20 years. But I never lost my affection for the patterns in the color plates of Bergman's book, and I still fish a number of them regularly. In part, this is no doubt sentimental, a reflection of the fact that they remind me of the unburdened days of my youth. But it is also utterly practical, because these drab assemblages of fur, peacock herl and mallard quill have accounted for many of my heaviest holdover trout.

So when the TDCs and *Callibaetis* patterns failed to produce so much as a swirl that morning, it wasn't at all out of character for me to tie on a Black Gnat. Constructed with a black chenille body, black cock or hen hackle and a gray duck quill wing, the Black Gnat isn't as "buggy" as other venerable wet flies like the Hare's Ear and the Leadwing Coachman. In fact, it is hard to know what trout mistake it for: A large chironomid? A drowned mayfly? An alderfly? An awful lot of trout have been fooled by Black Gnats over the years, however. I have read articles where Lee Wulff recommended it for grayling, and A.J. McClane claimed it was an excellent pattern for yellow perch. Clearly, the Black Gnat represents some subaquatic creature, probably a number of them.

I cast the fly along the shady side of an ancient cedar snag that had fallen into the lake at a right angle to the shoreline. I let the fly sink for a couple of beats, then worked it back toward the boat with a slow hand twist retrieve. The fish hit just as the fly passed over the drop-off into deeper water. When it felt the barb, it thrashed its head and barreled back into the lily pads—classic bass behavior. But then it jumped, revealing silver sides and a pink stripe. It was twice the size of the biggest trout I had ever taken from the lake.

When I slipped the hook from its mouth five minutes later, it filled the palm of my hand. It was an easy two pounds, maybe more. That isn't a big rainbow in many places, but it is a wonderful trout on the cold, basically infertile lakes of the coastal Northwest.

I had planned to keep a trout for dinner. I had a dozen morel mushrooms and a bunch of asparagus in the refrigerator at home. They are the traditional accompaniments to my first trout of the year. For me, the combination of steaming pink-fleshed trout, morels and asparagus is one springtime's most delightful rituals.

But this was obviously a holdover fish. It had gotten through the disorienting first few weeks in the lake after it was planted. It had also eluded all manner of predators—winged, finned, furred and with fly rods—for several years.

I opened my hand and watched it swim away. It was a survivor, after all.

Just like the Black Gnat.

During late April and May, the hike-in lakes at the 3,000- to 4,000-foot range in the Olympic Mountains gradually shed their husks of ice and snow. Unlike the peninsula's lowland lakes, which are nearly always ice-free year-round, these lakes are inaccessible much of the year. The natural history books refer to this tilted region of rocks and silver fir as the "montane zone." But I always think of the lakes at this elevation as "shoulder lakes," because they are incised onto the flanks of the mountains, a thousand feet below the tarns and cirque lakes of summer.

A fly fisherman I know that spends more time talking on the telephone about fishing than he does outdoors once told me that he doesn't fish mountain lakes because "all it is is *Callibaetis* and chironomids." That may be true on occasion, especially on some of the subalpine and alpine zone lakes, but many of the shoulder lakes are surprisingly fertile, with extensive weedy shallows and rocky shoals. The trout in these lakes feed not only on midges and mayflies, but also leeches, scuds, terrestrial insects, crayfish, and a host of other aquatic insects.

I tend to fish these lakes early in the season, most often when I am itching to see the high country again after a six-month absence. I usually hike up to two or three different lakes each spring, hoping to catch one of them at that magic moment when the water has warmed up a degree or two and the trout are feeding with abandon. Thinking it would be instructive to see how the trout activity and hatches played out on a specific body of water as springtime unfolded, however, I changed my approach last year. I hiked up to one of my favorite montane-zone lakes once a week for a month.

On opening day, I quickly switchbacked up past the trillium and bleeding heart blossoms at the trailhead and into the lower edge of the montane zone. Avalanche lilies and the mating hoots of blue grouse heralded the arrival of spring here, but drifts of snow lingered beneath the mountain hemlock. I hiked for another hour, then topped a final spur. The lake was three-fourths ice-free, but there was still four feet of snow around the inlet where I usually fished.

I used every cold-water technique I knew that day—twitching midge pupae up through the water column, scuttling Woolly Buggers across the bottom, fishing a mayfly nymph on a long leader. Nothing worked. Nothing worked the next week either, although mayflies and midges hovered above the water throughout the day. The ice was gone by the third week and there were only isolated patches of crusty, rotting snow in the shady places. I took two small brookies on a Black Gnat when alderflies swarmed over the bankside vegetation in late afternoon.

My wife Lisa joined me on my fourth climb up to the lake. It was mid-May now, the time of year I usually enjoy the best fishing of the year. I often take trout after trout on Zug Bugs and Gold Ribbed Hare's Ears off the inlet creek. But I couldn't buy a hit that day. Deciding to take a break, I walked back toward Lisa, who was sunning herself among a patch of marsh marigold near the outlet. I noticed several fish slashing through the water a few feet off the bank. Entirely on impulse, I snipped off my nymph and tied on a Leadwing Coachman.

John Alden Knight, originator of the *Solunar Tables*, writes that all the members of the coachman "genus" of flies trace their ancestry to the ancient Brown Hackle. For modern anglers, the connection between the Brown Hackle, Leadwing Coachman and the more widely-known Royal Coachman and Royal Wulff, seems tenuous at best. According to Knight, the patterns evolved like this: Tom Bosworth, a coachman for the British royal family, tied a Brown Hackle with a white wing, creating the Coachman; Scottish tiers substituted a starling wing, which became known as the Leadwing Coachman; the red silk and tail of the Royal Coachman were added by nineteenth century New York City tackle shop proprietor John Haily.

"Personally, I'll use any of them indiscriminately," Bergman wrote in *Trout* "and I'd feel lost without one or another in my box."

Whatever its provenence, I was fast to a fish less than a minute after I tied on the Leadwing Coachman. It was a vigorous, heavy fish, and it thrashed and slashed tirelessly beneath the surface. I didn't get a look at it until I eased it up into the grassy shallows. It was even bigger than I thought, nearly 14 inches long. Blue-circled red halos decorated its sides, and its orange fins were tipped with white. It wasn't a native to any watershed within a thousand miles, though, and my wife and I hadn't eaten a trout in six months.

When I cleaned the fish in our backyard, its flesh was as red as a sockeye salmon. Opening up its stomach, I found several scuds. That explained why flies with peacock herl bodies like the Zug Bug and the Leadwing Coachman worked so well on the lake. I also found a crayfish claw and, astonishingly, a full-grown salamander. The salamander was five and a half inches long, more than one-third the fish's length.

"This is going to taste great," I said, as I carried the fish into the kitchen. "It's been eating nothing but meat."

Two hours later, she agreed. "This is the best fish I've ever eaten," she said.

It's not all *Callibaetis* and chironomids.

Chapter 6 — Summer-Runs

From the half-pounders of the Klamath to the 20-pounders of the Skeena, and from the juniper and sage country of the Deschutes to the cedar and fir of the North Fork of the Stillaguamish, summer-run steelhead exert an almost gravitational pull over Northwestern fly fishing. Their willingness to move to the fly and their sizzling, incandescent struggles when hooked have made them the region's ultimate fly-rod fish. Flies like the Silver Hilton and Umpqua Special were originated for them. Techniques like waking and skating were developed with them in mind. And the Northwest's two most well-known fly fishermen—Zane Grey and Roderick Haig-Brown—are primarily remembered for their pursuit of summer-run steelhead.

It is for its winter steelhead that the Olympic Peninsula is most often celebrated, however. And rightly so, in my opinion, because the peninsula is home to the world's richest and most diverse assortment of winter steelhead water. The Salmon and Steelhead Stock Inventory released by the state and tribes in 1992 listed 49 stocks of Olympic Peninsula winter steelhead, but only 14 wild summer steelhead stocks. Even the peninsula's most famous fly fisherman, Syd Glasso, is best known for his pioneering work on winter steelhead.

Still, the half dozen large rivers that drain the west slope of the Olympics do host substantial runs of summer steelhead. And during my early years on the peninsula I explored the Sol Duc, Calawah and Bogachiel, the Hoh, Queets and Quinault during the summer. Over time, I fell into a routine. I fished the Sol Duc in June and early July, when early returning natives and its hatchery run of Skamania fish were in the river. In August, I spent time on the Hoh and Queets, then ended the season with a

climactic five- or six-day backpacking trip into the rain forest wilderness.

But there are a lot of ways for a fly fisherman to be pulled on the Olympic Peninsula during the summer—mountain lakes, the backcountry Elwha, the coast and the estuaries—and I probably only averaged about a dozen days a year fishing summer-runs.

That is, until about 10 years ago. I had a part-time job back then conducting interviews with saltwater sport fishermen as part of a research project for the National Marine Fisheries Service. Most of my assignments were on the eastern Strait of Juan de Fuca, Admiralty Inlet and Whidbey Island near my home in Port Townsend. But when I received my site list for that summer, nearly all of them were to places like Kalaloch, La Push, Neah Bay and Sekiu—right in the heart of West End steelhead country, in other words. It didn't take long for it to occur to me that this was a once-in-a-lifetime opportunity to immerse myself in summer steelhead fly fishing.

So, in what was perceived by many of my friends as the first flowering of a colossal middle age crisis, I gave up my apartment and made plans to spend the summer beside rivers. Actually, it didn't seem like that strange of a plan to me. Earlier in the year, I had to put my dog Darcy, boon companion for 16 years, to sleep. I was also divorced, without children. And I wasn't especially worried that the economic underpinnings of my life in Port Townsend—cobbled together by a bizarre yet stimulating combination of free-lance writing, music lessons, pizza making, gardening and the fishing interviews—couldn't be reassembled when the weather went south in late autumn.

It was with a sense of high excitement, then, that I filled my old rusted-out Toyota with camping gear, fly rods and books and headed west. I spent the first three days of my trip hunkered in my tent, waiting out a cold June rain. As the high water from the storm worked its way toward the ocean, however, the hatchery steelhead in the Sol Duc came to life. I caught two fish—a chunky eight-pounder and a feisty, tailwalking five pound buck—on Green Butt Skunks. It was a grand beginning to my adventure. And except for a day or two of early morning drizzle on the coastal valleys, it didn't rain again until after Labor Day.

I settled into a nice rhythm, moving between rivers and campsites more or less by whim. I usually got up early and fished for a couple of hours within walking distance of my tent. When I was on the Sol Duc, I worked the broken water at the head of a pool beneath a clay bank. I fished a lovely green run on the Calawah, and a section of shady pocket water on the Bogachiel. On days I had to work, I drove over to the trailer court in Beaver and used one of the public showers. When I didn't work, I either wrote or read my thrift shop copy of *Anna Karenina* during the afternoon. In the evenings, I gathered firewood, then scouted out new water into the gloaming.

It was a very simple and satisfying way to live. But after a month without rain, the Quillayute rivers were as low and clear as I had ever seen them. In fact, the sections of the river channels that had water in them were now actually smaller than the acres of bleached, stonefly-husk-adorned rocks they flowed through. I had the distinct feeling that all of the steelhead were up in the national park, holding in deep pools and off creek mouths. Other than a brief period at daybreak and at dusk, fishing was basically casting practice.

Then I had a five-day stretch without an assignment. I broke camp on the Sol Duc and headed south on 101. In Forks, I stocked up on ramen soup, Vienna sausages, cheese, and granola in the Shop-Rite, then crossed the street to Olympic Sporting Goods. I asked Bob Gooding, the store's proprietor, what shape he thought the rain forest rivers were in.

"Low, damned low," he said.

"Most of the snow's melted?" I asked.

Bob nodded emphatically. "Oh, hell yes," he said. "They're clear. Real clear."

Known throughout the world for its unique, temperate-zone rain forests, the West End of the Olympic Peninsula, nonetheless, experiences a sort of mini-drought during late summer and early fall. Indeed, although the Hoh, Queets and Quinault valleys receive up to 12 feet of rain annually, the heaviest in the contiguous United States, more than 75 percent of that rain falls between October and April. In typical years, less than 10 inches of rain falls during summer. Visitors to the peninsula are often amazed that dusk covers the salal and fern understory, the boughs of the cedar trees droop, and small tributary creeks are bone dry.

Because they rise on glaciers rather than on snowfields like the Quillayute rivers, however, the rain forest rivers maintain good flows even during the driest summers. Moreover, the bed load of pulverized rock known as glacial flour keeps them from becoming too clear. Extended periods of hot weather can cause the glaciers themselves to bleed into the rivers, resulting in high, opaque-gray water. But if you hit them after the previous winter's snowfall has melted and while the temperatures are in the 70s, the Hoh, Queets and Quinault are usually the best late summer show in town.

Of the three rain forest rivers, I chose the Queets. In recent years, a visit to a rain forest valley has become an integral part of every Olympic Peninsula visitor's itinerary. And the Hoh Valley on the north and the Quinault Valley on the south offer the sort of services that urban and suburban sensibilities tend to demand. Not surprisingly, the campgrounds fill early and the concessionaires and ranger stations are busy all day. Even the trails are often crowded, as climbers head toward Mount Olympus and hikers aim for Low Divide or Enchanted Valley.

The section of the Queets Valley outside the Quinault Indian Reservation, on the other hand, has no amenities. There is no ranger station. There is no dump station. There is no place to use a credit card or a calling card. Not surprisingly, this southwestern leg of the national park is one of the least-visited areas of the peninsula. Indeed, the only vehicular access to the area is along the Queets River Road, a low-speed, low-maintenance gravel road that parallels the south bank of the river for 13 miles, then dead-ends at a rustic park service campground. Beyond there, the only way to travel upriver is on the trail on the north side of the river.

That's right. The trail is on the opposite side of the river from the campground. To get to it, you must wade the broad, fast, slick-bottomed river, while carrying a heavy pack on your back. It's no cakewalk of a wade, either. I am about 5 feet 10 inches tall, weigh around 185 and have a good sense of balance. But every time I have forded the Queets there has come a moment when I felt I had lost control of the situation and was at the complete mercy of the current. I've always made it. I've never heard of anyone who hasn't, but, believe me, it will get your blood going, even during the lowest water of the year.

This day wasn't any different. I crammed the supplies into the pouch of my old Kelty backpack, then tied my hiking boots to the top and laced up my wading shoes. I shouldered the pack and heeled down the path that leads to Sams River, a tributary to the Queets. After rock-hopping across the stream, I found a stout cottonwood limb to complement my rod tube as a wading staff. I unfastened the waist belt on my pack next, so I could jettison it quickly if I fell. Then I waded into the safest-looking spot I could find.

I moved quickly but purposefully, digging in with my staffs. I concentrated on maintaining contact with the bottom. Before

I had expected, I was up to my waist. I wondered if I had chosen a bad place to cross. Idiotically, I tried to remember if my granola was in the bottom of the pack where it would get wet. By now, my legs were numb, and I felt as though I had lost purchase with the bottom. I could feel the current digging the gravel from beneath my feet, and I was aware that I was moving downstream nearly as much as I was across. But then I realized I was more than half way to the other side. I sloshed the last 30 feet to shore like a boxer in the 15th round of a split decision.

I sat on a patch of gray sand and ate a handful of gorp while my feet dried. Watching the shifting patterns of light and energy play through the green water was mesmerizing, as it has been since I was a boy. I could have sat there all afternoon, but two-thirds of the day's light was already gone. I pulled on my hiking socks and boots and wriggled the heavy pack up onto my back. I headed up the trail.

Winding 15 miles upstream to Pelton Creek, the Queets Trail passes through one of the Northern Hemisphere's most magnificent forests. Cathedral-like groves of Sitka spruce and hemlock filter the summer sun into mottled shafts of diffused light. Big leaf maple wear splendid raiments of licorice fern and club moss. Fallen logs give conifer seedlings a foothold above the forest floor, while arrow-straight rows of mature trees known as colonnades testify to the presence of forgotten nurse logs. Despite the dense, luxuriant canopy of trees, the forest is surprisingly open. Large resident elk herds crop the huckleberry, oxalis and fern understory, creating the park-like feeling that distinguishes the Olympic rain forests from other Northwestern river valleys.

I hiked for about two hours, then dumped my pack next to an immense Sitka spruce. I could have gone farther, all the way to the steelhead boundary at Tshletshy Creek, but I had camped in this same glade before, had used these same fire-blackened rocks to cook over on other trips. I took a long swig from my water bottle—for some reason I don't like to drink while I am on the trail—then I set up my tent and spread out my sleeping pad and bag. I walked down to the river and filled a couple of bottles with water. Then I gathered a spine-wrenching armful of driftwood for the night's fire.

It was about eight o'clock. The sun had tracked far to the west, out over the ocean, and shadows crept across the long, boulder-studded section of pocket water I intended to fish. I pulled on my summer-weight waders, laced up my canvas wading shoes and grabbed my 7-weight. As I walked across the wide gravel bar, clouds of small caddisflies hovered above the water, along with an occasional graceful mayfly spinner and high-flying Yellow Sally. With the hot sun off the river bottom, the bar now had a rich, heavy swampy smell, that heady mixture of water and approaching night.

Inspired by Bill McMillan's book *Dry Line Steelhead*, I had been fishing floating patterns like Bombers, Muddler Minnows and large Wulffs almost exclusively the last few weeks on the Quillayute rivers. On the Queets, though, the glacial color made floating flies a little less likely a prospect than on the clear-flowing, snowmelt streams. So I selected the spool with my sink tip and tied on an old standby—a black Woolly Bugger. Like most fly fishermen, I don't know if I catch more fish with my pet patterns because I fish them more often and with more confidence or because they are actually better flies. If pressed, I guess I would say I do well with the Woolly Bugger because it represents a host of creatures.

I decided to make a few casts downstream of the mouth of a small tributary creek before working the pocket water. I had never caught anything from the shallow gravelly chute and, to tell you the truth, I couldn't understand why steelhead would hold there. After all, the water from the creek couldn't be as cold as the mainstem river's glacier water, which is the most common reason fish hang below feeder creeks.

Also, there is deeper and more broken water out in the main river. But I had seen three summer steelhead, their gray shadows moving sinuously with the current, hanging below the creek mouth the summer before.

Could this be where the fish had emerged from the spawning gravel four or five years earlier, I wondered? Could they have been pulled across thousands of miles of tractless seas and past scores of seemingly identical feeder creeks to this nameless brook? Will they hang in this thin water till winter, like iron filings before a magnet? I knew it was possible, perhaps even likely. But like all of the great mysteries of this planet, it tested belief.

I cast across the creek and let the current carry the fly down into the river like a dislodged nymph. When the fly began to hang downstream, I stripped back sharply on the line. I wasn't particularly surprised when I felt resistance, thinking it was probably a snag. But suddenly I felt a head shake. Then a steelhead thrashed on the surface.

I struck back instinctively. Feeling the hook, the fish streaked downstream 30 feet into the deeper water of the main channel. It jumped three times. They were rapid-fire, somersaulting leaps. The flawless silver sides of the steelhead glimmered in the watery shadows. It was at least a 10-pound fish.

I leaned back on the rod tentatively, but the steelhead shook its head and raced across to the far side of the river. I walked downstream, carefully retrieving any line I regained. But then it swam back upstream and jumped again. It took back all of the line I had respooled. The wrist of my rod hand was beginning to hurt.

Ten minutes later—and within 15 feet of a stretch of fast water where I would in all likelihood have lost the fish instantly—I tailed it up onto the beach. It was a gorgeous fish, a narrow-waisted, thick-shouldered buck so fresh from the sea its scales were still partially loose. Even in the fading summer light, I could see the feathered, translucent perfection of its adipose and ventral fins. I slipped the barbless hook from its mouth and eased it head first back into the current. I expected to nurse it for a few moments while it regained its equilibrium, but it shot out of my palms.

I stood up straight and stretched. My shoulders and neck were stiff, my wrist was nearly numb and a blister was forming on my thumb. But I was smiling. This, after all, was why I had spent the last two months sleeping on the ground. It is also why summer steelhead have been the brilliant, fixed points of light that Northwestern fly fishing has revolved around for more than a century.

Summer steelhead seek the shady riffles of the backcountry in late summer.

Chapter 7

Bug
Factories

Red bunchberries had sprawled across the forest floor and chanterelle mushrooms hid under moldering blowdown the last time I followed the overgrown skidder trail down to the beaver pond. I had carried a paper sack in the back pocket of my fly vest then and my grandfather's side-by-side 12 gauge. They weren't entirely fanciful gestures. One glorious October afternoon, I shot a grouse, filled a sack with mushrooms and caught a half-dozen cutthroat and brookies within a quarter mile of the pond.

It was early summer now, and the bunchberry's delicate white flowers brightened the duff, along with twin flower and false lily of the valley. It is a short walk to the pond, but the last 20 yards or so snake through a dense understory of huckleberry and alder. I walked bent over and carried my rod behind me. I could hear the chatter of the creek below the dam. When I emerged from the brush, three mallards blew out of the cattails on the far side of the pond. They climbed quickly through the dawn fog that hung over the small valley.

In October, the pond had been low, with the creek channel clearly discernible through emergent vegetation. After a wet Northwestern winter, however, it sprawled across the small basin and lapped at the top of the stick and mud dam. Lily pads and cattails were the only plants visible in the high dark water.

There was no surface activity. In fact, unless you knew better, it would be easy to conclude that the pond was fishless. One of the curious things about even the most productive beaver ponds is that they just don't look like what we have been conditioned to think of as trout water. Murky, rank with decaying vegetation and crosshatched with flooded brush and timber, beaver ponds seem more like Everglades sloughs than trout habitat.

I knew better. Indeed, during the last three years, I had caught and released dozens of wild cutthroat and brook trout from this pond. Most of them were in the eight- to 12-inch range, but I had also taken several natives of around 15 inches and a beautiful 17-inch brookie that pushed the three-pound mark. Perhaps most important of all, I had never been skunked.

I tied on a number 8 black Woolly Bugger. From past experience, I knew that I could take a few trout early in the morning from the deep water along the face of the dam. Curiously, these dawn trout are always brookies, and they are always in the deepest water. I have no explanation for this. During the entire rest of the day, regardless of the time of year or where you fish, you take five or six cutthroat for every brookie. Only in the first gray awakening of the day do the eastern transplants predominate. I often wonder about this when I am on the water, but I always forget to bring it up when I am talking to a biologist. Maybe brook trout simply get up earlier than cutthroat.

After I tested my knot, I climbed up on a large snag that angles from the bank out into the water. Even a fair caster can reach the other side of the pond here—that is, you could if you had the room for a backcast. But both sides of the pond are hemmed tightly with alders and conifers. The bottom also drops off too sharply at this end of the pond for wading. By standing on the snag, however, you can arc your backcast up into an opening between the tops of the brush and the lowest limbs of the trees, then snap the line down and out over the water. It's an ugly sort of casting stroke, but it works. And I have done it often enough that I now know where the opening is without having to look.

My first cast fell a foot or so short of the dam. I paused for a few seconds, letting the heavy fly sink, then retrieved it with gentle six-inch strips. Almost immediately, I felt the tug of a fish, a nice sharp tug. I jerked back twice on the rod. The fish wanted to stay on the bottom and slug it out, but I worked it to the surface. It splashed furiously. It was only about 10 inches long, but it put a nice bend in my 6-weight. I jumped off the snag and led it towards shore. For about the thousandth time, it occurred to me that brook trout are one of the most beautiful things on the planet. I released it.

By now, a few small trout had begun to pick off emerging midges with their characteristically exuberant rises. I reeled my fly line in and waded through the soupy, algae-rich water down to the thick row of cattails that extended three-fourths of the way across the pond. Three years earlier, when I had stumbled onto the beaver pond, a four-foot high dam had blocked the creek where the cattails now grew. But it had blown out during the winter, and when I returned the following opening day the beavers had built the new dam 50 yards downstream.

I knew where the old dam lay, though. For the last couple of years it had given me access to the deepest part of the channel and served as a rickety but serviceable casting platform. Unfortunately, it was gradually rotting away under the water. So as I picked my way along the top of the dam, I held onto cattails with my free hand and carefully sought out a solid foothold before putting my weight on it. On more than one occasion it has occurred to me that I am probably more likely to get hurt fishing a beaver pond than the more dramatic places I fish, like glacial rivers or the rocky surf.

When I finally got into position, I snipped off the Woolly Bugger and lengthened my tippet. I tied on a size 14 Gold Ribbed Hare's Ear. A number 14 fly, of course, is too big to represent most midges. But it is a rough representation of a

Callibaetis nymph. And although these still-water mayflies wouldn't emerge for several hours, I had learned the beaver-pond trout fed heavily on the nymphs on early summer mornings.

I caught a half-dozen cutthroat as the fog burned off and the sky turned from close and gray to high and blue. I didn't catch a fish on every cast, and none of the trout were over a foot long. It wasn't easy fishing, either. The near side of the deep water where the creek broke through the old dam was at the comfortable end of my casting ability, while the far side was attainable only if I muscled it. Moreover, if I dropped my arm on the backcast, I snagged the picket line of cattails behind me. But when I managed to drop my fly into the sweet spot, I usually hooked a fish.

After the large brown mayflies began to appear on the surface, I stopped getting as many hits. Then the action stopped altogether. I could have put on a dry fly, but in the past I had only taken small beaver-pond trout on floating patterns. I replaced the beige fly with a pale green one—a damselfly nymph.

During June, great numbers of damselfly nymphs swim from deep water toward shore, where they crawl up on cattail stalks, lily pads and floating logs and emerge. Swimming only a few inches from the surface, the slender, three-tailed nymphs are very vulnerable to trout. They are also a mouthful. Nearly all of the larger trout I have taken from the pond have fallen to a damselfly nymph.

This day wasn't an exception. On my second cast, there was a prodigious swirl beneath my leader. Striking back instinctively, I set the hook. The fish splashed on the surface, revealing the amber flanks of a cutthroat, then dashed for the lily pads. For several minutes it was touch and go as the fish tried to break off on every stick-up, cattail and snag it could find. But my 5X tippet held, and I slipped my hand under a chunky 14-inch trout. It was heavily spotted below the lateral line, like all coastal cutthroat, but it had the dark shading of a resident fish, one that had never been to sea. I released it.

Each year, as the first of June draws near, I face the same dilemma: Do I drive out to the Hoh or Sol Duc and try for an early-returning summer-run steelhead? Or do I spend opening day of the river fishing season on one of the beaver ponds in the swampy lowlands between the foothills of the eastern Olympics and Hood Canal?

I usually head south. For one thing, the weather on the peninsula in early June is unpredictable—and so are the river conditions. Two years ago, for example, I spent a couple of days in late May squiring a film crew around the upper Hoh. We had a cool dry spring and the river was in absolutely terrific shape for fly fishing—low and clear, but with enough color to keep the fish from being too spooky. But the temperature climbed into the low 80s the day before the opener. The Hoh looked good as I back-packed up into the rain forest, but I was worried. And, sure enough, the river was roaring with glacial melt when I woke up the next day. I didn't even wet a line.

In addition, although steelhead are currently the hottest, most written about fish in angling—with coffee table books, glossy specialty magazines, videos, celebrities and the fawning Boswells to chronicle their exploits—I can fish for steelhead 11 months of the year on the peninsula. So in a way that probably seems incomprehensible to someone who lives in, say, Colorado or Pennsylvania, steelhead are my bread and butter fish. On the other hand, I can only fish for trout in beaver ponds between June 1 and the end of October. Consequently, I begin to daydream about native cutthroat and wild brookies as the opener draws near.

I also like beaver ponds because they are bug factories. Much of the fishing on the peninsula consists of trying to tempt fish that aren't hungry into hitting flies that don't resemble much of anything. And even when you move from the anadromous fish rivers to the streams and stillwaters that hold resident populations of trout, most Olympic fish are not particularly selective. There are exceptions—mountain lakes; the backcountry sections of the Elwha; Price's Lake. But for the most part, Olympic Peninsula fly fishermen have few opportunities to engage in the elaborate dance of hatch (and nymph) matching that enthralls anglers in other parts of the country.

This isn't because the trout are stupid. Rather, Olympic rivers tend to be steep, fast and cold, just as the peninsula's lakes are usually cold and without large insect-producing shoal areas. Moreover, the very medium the trout live in—the peninsula's water—falls on the tough luck side of the pH scale. Compared to fish in the insect-rich, alkaline waters of the Columbia Basin and Rocky Mountains, Olympic Peninsula resident trout live a hardscrabble sort of existence. They grab food wherever and whenever they can get it.

When beavers dam a small creek, however, the pond behind it becomes a veritable petri dish for the propagation of sub-aquatic life. Indeed, beaver ponds have the characteristics of both a stream and a lake, and stillwater insects like dragonflies and damselflies flourish alongside river-dwellers like *Tricorythodes*. Most beaver ponds are on the small side, as well, so terrestrial insects routinely become part of the nutritional stew. Non-insects like leeches, scuds, crayfish and amphibians round out the menu. About the only traditional trout food that you don't usually find in beaver ponds are stoneflies.

Trout lucky enough to live upstream of a beaver dam tend to eat better than their counterparts in small rivers and lakes. But that is not their only advantage. The dam also slows the speed of the current through the pond. This enables the trout to expend less energy than their relatives downstream, which, in turn, allows them to grow larger more quickly. Finally, the slower water gives the fish more time to look their food over before striking. This makes them more selective.

Those are the logical reasons for why I usually head to a beaver pond on opening day. But the most compelling reason of all is completely subjective: I just feel good when I am up to my waist in a beaver pond. In their own way, they are as riotously, extravagantly alive as the rocky coast. I like the way they smell, that rich, peppery decaying-vegetable-matter fecundity. I like the fact that the trout in them are almost always wild. I like the way that I have to find them by checking out rumors and hunches and sloshing up narrow, tangled feeder creeks. And I like the fact that I am almost always blessedly alone on a beaver pond.

Robert Traver, patron saint of beaver-pond fly fishermen and author of *Trout Madness* and *Anatomy of a Murder*, put it this way: "Perhaps it is only one man's small rebellion against this whole tedious bigger-and-better philosophy as it more and more afflicts our outdoors, indeed our very life..."

A deeply spotted, beaver pond cutthroat trout.

Chapter 8

Stoneflies

If you have an attachment to normal sleep patterns, it is impossible to fish both dawn and dusk on West End rivers during midsummer. Located a few degrees either side of the 48th parallel, the northern part of the Olympic Peninsula is about as far north as you can get in the lower 48 states. The peninsula's maritime climate, of course, is much milder than places like Kalispell, the Boundary Waters or northern Maine at the same latitude, but even the Japanese Current can't alter the path of the sun. During late June and early July, it is light enough to fish before 5 a.m. and it doesn't get dark until nearly 10:00 at night.

So after two days of dawn and dusk fishing on the Bogachiel River, my inclination was to hang around camp and go to bed early. I had begun each day fishing the pocket water in front of my camp for steelhead. Once the sun topped the line of cottonwoods on the opposite side of the river, I exchanged my waders for hiking boots and bushwhacked upstream for four or five miles. A drenching summer rain and big summer high tides the week before had pulled in a strong, early run of sea-run cutthroat and I found them in just about every shady pool. I didn't usually get back to camp until early evening, when I fished the pockets for steelhead again.

But that night I wanted to cook an early dinner, then mess around with the *New York Times* crossword puzzle from the *Seattle Post Intelligencer* I had bought in Forks. As I snapped twigs for kindling, however, I noticed a number of large—very large—insects hovering above the river. Since it was too late in the year for salmonflies and too early for October caddis, I knew they could only be one thing: golden stoneflies. I could see the swirls and rolls of fish rising to the egg-laying females.

Shaking off my fatigue, I pulled on my waders and crossed the gravel bar to the river. The sun dipped a finger beneath the tops of the cottonwood as I waded into position at the head of the pocket water. Now the entire complement of Northwestern subaquatic insects—mayflies, a sifting of midges, awkwardly flying caddisflies, Yellow Sallies—was backlit in the streaky Northern twilight. Dwarfing them all, the golden stones lumbered through the air like over-burdened freight helicopters.

I added a couple of feet to my leader and knotted on a yellow Stimulator. Normally, dry flies don't come into their own on the large West End streams until after the golden stones have come and gone. In June and early July, the rivers tend to be high and cold, sometimes higher than during late winter and early spring. Sink tips and wet flies, consequently, are usually the most productive tackle. But we had yet another dry spring and early summer that year, and the Bogachiel was low and a couple of degrees warmer than usual. Moreover, with the early show of cutthroat, there was an alternate target if steelhead refused to look toward the surface. I figured this might be my best chance ever to take a fish on a dry fly during the golden stone hatch.

I quartered the cast down- and across-stream, placing it just above the apron of soft water behind a large rock. As the fly floated into the pocket, I extended the rod across my body and increased tension on the fly with my line hand. The Stimulator kicked up a little furrow as it cut slowly across the grain of the current. I let it hang limply downstream for a moment at the end of the drift, then carefully retrieved my line. I cast again, then again.

On the fourth swing, the fly had

tracked about 10 feet when I saw a white mouth beneath it. Startled, I dropped the line at the exact moment the fish slashed at the fly. I jerked back with the rod. I felt the fish for a second, but then it spit out the fly. As if to tease me, as if to give me a glimpse of what my incompetence had prevented me from experiencing, the fish rolled on the surface. I could see the dark back and pewter sides of a large summer-run steelhead.

For the next 15 minutes, I tried every follow-up technique and trick I could remember. The only responses I had were from a juvenile steelhead and a chunky Chinook smolt. Then I was suddenly very weary. I waded back to shore. A kingfisher ratcheted querulously from a snag downstream. A few golden stones still dipped toward the darkening water.

In terms of total biomass, stoneflies are probably the second most abundant insect on the large glacial and snowmelt streams of the Olympic Peninsula, surpassed only by caddisflies. The salmonflies, which usually begin to hatch in mid-April, and the golden stoneflies, June or early July emergers, are two of the largest insects in Olympic rivers, as much as two inches long as adults. Because these species have multi-year nymphal stages, they provide trout and juvenile steelhead and salmon with a year-round food source. In addition, the smaller green and yellow stoneflies are present in bewildering profusion from within a roll cast of tidewater to the headwater canyons. On sunny winter afternoons, small black stoneflies hover over West End steelhead streams.

Yet stonefly patterns have never held much currency with Northwestern fly fishermen. In Montana, you could conceivably run a guiding operation with nothing but Golden Stones, Box Canyon Stones and Sofa Pillows. Anglers are equally enamored of Plecoptera on the red-rock canyons of Colorado rivers like the Gunnison and on Central Oregon's sun-blasted Deschutes. But in the fern and fog country of the coastal Northwest, where the rivers are principally nurseries and reproductive arenas for migratory fish, fly patterns have traditionally been more fanciful than representative. This has changed somewhat in recent years, as more of the life history of steelhead has become known to anglers. But a glance at the steelhead patterns in any of the region's more influential fly fishing mail order catalogs reveals only one pattern that makes any claim to a living creature—the October Caddis.

Why is this? The conventional wisdom has always maintained that it isn't necessary to cast representative patterns for steelhead because the fish don't feed on their spawning runs. But that raises an even larger question: Why do steelhead hit flies or lures or bait at all? Over the years, many theories have been offered to explain why these nonfeeding fish provide such a dependable sport fishery. One maintains that steelhead strike out of anger, that they are territorial and automatically attack anything that crowds them. Another theory claims that the fish hit objects out of curiosity. Both of these explanations are certainly correct at least part of the time, and they account for the enduring popularity and productivity of bright, non-representative patterns like the Skykomish Sunrise and Purple Peril. These flies catch the eye of steelhead even in rain-swollen winter flows.

But why are black patterns like Skunks and drab patterns like Muddler Minnows also enduringly productive? It has been speculated that black patterns do well because they contrast with the predominately gray-green stream bottoms of most Northwestern rivers. But is that the only reason? After all, any angler who has cleaned more than a few steelhead can tell you that it is not uncommon to encounter nymphs, adult insects and crustaceans in their stomachs. Biologists say that this is because these organisms have triggered the fish's "strike reflex," the instinct left over from the fish's days of feeding in the river as a juvenile and later at sea.

This reflex, no doubt, accounts for the success of floating patterns like Stimulators and buggy subsurface flies like Muddlers. It also explains the effectiveness of shrimp and prawn imitations like the General Practitioner. I believe, similarly, that large black (and occasionally brown) patterns are consistently productive on Olympic Peninsula streams because they represent stonefly nymphs tumbling in the drift.

I am far from the first person to think adult anadromous fish target stoneflies on occasion. In an article in *Gray's Sporting Journal*, Lee Wulff described fishing a stonefly-inspired pattern for Atlantic salmon as far back as 1947. And in their definitive work, *Stoneflies*, Richards, Swisher and Arbona devote an entire chapter to fishing dry stonefly patterns for Atlantic salmon. "...the type of streams Atlantic salmon are usually found in is perfect habitat for large stoneflies, and the years that the immature salmon spend in the home water before going to sea must entail many meals of natural stoneflies."

On this side of the Continental Divide, steelhead fly fishermen with an interest in stoneflies usually concentrated on the subsurface phase of the insect's life. During the 1970s, floating line guru Bill McMillan perfected a technique for tumbling heavily-weighted stonefly nymphs on the tributaries to the lower Columbia. At roughly the same time, James Garrett, the Washington Department of Fisheries employee who eventually became the founding president of the peninsula chapter of the Federation of Fly Fishermen, created a series of stoneflies for the faster, heavier waters of the North Olympic Peninsula.

Garrett's stonefly nymphs are marvels, faithful to the original insect to a degree seldom seen in steelhead flies, yet also graced with breathtaking artistry. They are displays of technique and imagination that approach sorcery. They also catch fish. Gradually, like a freshet that revives the pulse of a late September stream, Garrett's flies—and his reputation—became the talk of the local fly

fishing community. It was obvious that at long last, the Olympic Peninsula had an heir to Syd Glasso.

I can remember the first time I fished a Garret-inspired stonefly nymph. It was mid-April. We had a big, sloppy French kiss of a snowstorm in late March, with snow sluicing off the Sitka spruce and red cedar boughs almost as quickly as it fell. The next three days were dry, but they were followed by 10 days of rain, mist and drizzle. I didn't have to call Gene Owens at the Westward Hoh to know that the rain forest rivers were out. And Bob Gooding told me to forget the Bogey. I thought about the Dickey and the Calawah. But, as I nearly always do when I worry about river conditions, I ended up on the Sol Duc.

It was in good shape, too, a luminescent, lime-pulp green. I picked up a cup of coffee at the Sappho Cafe, drove to a spot above the river where I parked my truck, then scrambled through a quarter mile of crumbling, moss-covered blow down. The willows along the river were three feet above my head, and as I bucked through them I felt something crawling on my neck. Swiping instinctively, I captured a large, writhing creature. It had approximately the same size and heft of a spark plug. It was a salmonfly—*Pteronarcys californica*. Opening my hand slowly, I peered at the delicate venation on its wings and its orange thorax. I tossed it into the air and watched it fly away.

My plan had been to fish bright wet flies on short leaders with sink tips, a good strategy on Olympic rivers in March and April. But I kicked up a small cloud of salmonflies as I pushed through the willows. The larger rocks along the river bank were also covered with amber gray nymphal husks. So I sat on a moss-covered boulder and replaced the sink tip spool on my reel with a floater. I had fished stoneflies in the Gardiner and Gallatin and Yellowstone in Montana, as well as in Colorado and Oregon, and I didn't figure there was any reason to do it any differently on the Sol

Duc. I added two feet to my leader and tied on a nymph that a friend of mine had tied after taking a class from Garrett at the community college.

I cast slightly upstream, along the outside edge of the main current. Following the fly downstream with the rod and mending line to keep it drag free. I focused on the narrow tip of the double taper. Suddenly, the line jumped upstream. I reared back on the rod and yanked slack with my left hand. It turned out to be a juvenile salmon, about eight inches long. Two casts later, I hooked a resident cutthroat of about 10 inches. These weren't steelhead, but I had a grin on my face. A few minutes later, I caught and released another salmon.

I extended my line a couple of feet into the body of the current. The fly bounced along the bottom for about 10 yards. There was a slight tug as I lifted the rod at the end of the drift. Jerking back quickly, I felt resistance, that heavy, pulsing live sensation of a fish. Moments later, a steelhead thrashed violently on the surface, then jumped. I saw its faint red strip, its dark back and thick tail. It raced 20 yards downstream to the thin water of the tailout and jumped again. The fly fell from its mouth.

Since then, black stonefly nymphs have become one of my standard patterns on Olympic rivers. I often begin the day swinging Garrett-inspired nymphs through pocket water on a dead-drift. That's a demanding

way to fish, though, and once my concentration begins to waver, I switch to more generic black patterns like Woolly Buggers or leeches. I fish them on a sink tip with a swing, a technique where I feel I have more control than a dead-drift. In early summer, I fish golden stone nymphs at least part of the time. But to tell you the truth, I have never had as much luck with the lighter patterns, and I usually fall back on black pretty quickly. Perhaps this is simply because the golden stones are not as abundant as salmonflies on West End rivers.

As for the steelhead that hit the Stimulator on the Bogachiel—well, as I have said before, timing is everything on the peninsula. I haven't encountered low, warm water during a heavy golden stone hatch very often since then. And I have never tempted another summer steelhead to a dry fly during the hatch. I keep trying, though. I even fish dry flies during the salmonfly hatch from time to time.

One time, I mentioned to a friend how weird it seemed that we have these incredible hatches year after year that the adult fish basically ignore.

"The little fish pay attention," was his reply.

I thought about the white mouth and tantalizing roll of the Bogachiel summer-run. My friend was right: The little fish do pay attention. And the big fish sometimes remember.

Chapter 9

The Last
Wilderness

"Damnit," I said to my friend Seth Stephens. "I think I forgot the scuds."

"This probably isn't the best time to remember that," Seth replied.

We had just hiked six miles into the Buckhorn Wilderness Area in the northeastern corner of the Olympic Mountains. The last mile had been a nearly vertical pitch up a sun-blasted scree slope. Now we stood on the lip of a small glacial cirque. Sprawling below us, a subalpine tarn reflected the flawless blue of the summer sky. Although it was mid-July and the temperature was in the 80s, dirty patches of snow still clung to the north-facing walls of the talus slopes above us. A few scraggly subalpine firs grew around the edge of the lake, but at 6,000 feet we were right at the edge of the tree line.

Seth is one of the nicest men I know—gentle and considerate, the kind of guy that genuinely empathizes with you when you mess something up. But he was planning on fishing hardware on this trip, and I don't think he could truly appreciate the disaster it was that I left the Trueblood's Otter Shrimp at home. Unlike most stillwater sub-aquatic insects, which are only available to trout fleetingly, the small, freshwater crustaceans known as scuds are a year-round, high protein mouthful in the lakes they inhabit. "Seldom do you encounter a high elevation lake that turns out trout over 20 inches that doesn't have a scud population," Randall Kauffman and Ron Cordes state in their excellent book *Lake Fishing with a Fly*. Scuds were one of the main reasons Seth and I had decided to fish the lake.

Atlantic salmon were the other reason. Planted into the lake a number of years before by the Washington Department of Game, the salmon had thrived in the isolated, backcountry lake. Indeed, at the time of our hike, the state record Atlantic salmon was from the lake, a 6 3/4-pounder taken by an Olympic Peninsula angler. Rumor had it that the lake had been chosen for the salmon because of its remoteness and the presence of the scuds. There is no natural reproduction in the lake, however, and stocking had been discontinued due to a lack of funds. Seth and I wanted to try mountain-lake salmon fishing before the final generation of fish died out.

So I had planned to fish scud patterns. But now, after an initial frantic grabbing search of my pack, followed by a superficially calm ordered search of each pocket and compartment, I could clearly picture the small film canister of scud patterns on my writing desk. With a feeling more like dread than optimism, I flipped open the top of my small "backpacking" fly box.

"Have you got anything close?" Seth asked.

One half of the small aluminum box held dry flies—Royal and Grizzly Wulffs I used on fast mountain streams like the Dungeness and Graywolf; Elk Hair Caddis for the backcountry Elwha; and a selection of Griffith's Gnats to use as chironomid emergers. But I needed a subsurface pattern to imitate a scud, so my gaze shifted over to the other side of the box. There, resting snugly in their clips were Black Gnats and Gold Ribbed Hare's Ears, TDCs and Zug Bugs. And a handful of damselfly nymphs.

"Well, it's a stretch," I said, lifting a size 14 Zug Bug from the box. "But I've taken fish on it in scud water before."

I put the fly back in the box, and Seth and I shouldered our packs again. We followed a well-beaten footpath toward the inlet where a rill from the snowfields above drained into the lake. Surrounded by pink flowering heather and low mats of juniper, it was a perfect place for a campsite.

We were about halfway there when Seth suddenly stopped. "Look," he said, excitedly. He pointed toward the water.

I could see three torpedo-shaped fish moving together about 10 feet off shore. They were all in the 20-inch size range.

"Jesus," I said. "Look at them."

"Makes that hike seem worth it, doesn't it?"

We watched the fish until they swam out of sight. We both wanted to drop the packs and begin fishing right away. But there is an unspoken protocol among backpackers that you don't play around until camp has been made. We carried the packs the rest of the way to the inlet. We saw another school of five salmon of about the same size. Like the first fish, they moved as a group a few yards off shore.

Finally, after setting up the tent, spreading out our pads and sleeping bags and gathering firewood (this was before it was illegal to have fires at that altitude), we were set. Seth grabbed his box of spinners and spoons and took off for the north end of the lake. I hiked around to the southeast shore.

Midges rose sporadically from the surface, and a few mayfly spinners bobbed elegantly through the thin mountain air. No fish were rising, though, so I threaded a floating line and long leader through my guides and tied on the Zug Bug. With a 40-foot cast, about two-thirds of the retrieve was through blind water. I retrieved the fly with the short, uneven starts that are supposed to imitate scuds.

I noticed a pair of salmon cruising in from the right just as the fly came back into view. Like the other fish, they maintained an invisible counterclockwise circuit around the lake. I slowed my retrieve, timing it to intercept the fish. With mounting excitement, I watched them narrow the distance. Suddenly, they were just a rod length from the fly. I stripped six inches of line, bringing the nymph directly across their sight line. I could see the fly hang before them in the

clear mountain water, then flutter toward the bottom. The fish stared at it briefly, but they didn't miss a beat.

As I worked my way around the south side of the lake, I saw several other small groups of fish. They all worked the same clockwork pattern around the inside edge of the lake's shoal water. None of them so much as turned their heads at my fly. I was still optimistic—when you can actually see big fish, it's hard not to be—but I kept thinking about the scud patterns back home.

I tried a Gold Ribbed Hare's Ear next. I hadn't been able to find any live scuds in the lake, and I figured they might be more gray-brown than green. Also, the Gold Ribbed Hare's Ear is a fairly accurate representation of the nymphal form of the *Callibaetis* mayflies that bobbed above the lake. I didn't really suspect that fish the size of the salmon spent much time popping mayfly nymphs. But I figured a fly that looked sort of like two food sources might overcome their resistance. It didn't.

By now, the sun had sunk below the ridgeline to the west. Shadows played across the surface of the lake, and I could no longer see into the water. An enormous chironomid hatch boiled off the surface film. Without so much as a single surface rise, however, fishing a midge seemed rather pointless. I could see Seth casting and retrieving at the other end of the lake, his metal lure glinting in the gathering twilight.

Deciding to give up on scuds, I beefed up my tippet and tied on a Marabou Muddler. I cast as far as I could, waited for the fly to sink, then inched it in slowly with fits and starts. I was trying to imitate a crayfish. For some inexplicable reason, fishing blind now made me more hopeful. At least, I couldn't see the damned things refuse my fly. Unfortunately, the Muddler had the same effect as all my other patterns, which was no effect at all.

By now, Seth had returned to camp and was assembling a fire. Just ten more minutes, I told myself. I tried a chartreuse Woolly Worm for a few casts. Finally, just before it became too dark to fish, I tried the floating line and Zug Bug again.

The lambent orange of the campfire was welcoming as I walked back to camp. In the darkness, the peaks above seemed even taller. The patches of snow gave off a brittle blue light.

"Any bites?" Seth asked, as I hopped across the creek.

"Nah. How about you?"

I tossed a couple of new logs on the fire, while Seth fiddled with his Primus stove.

"I saw quite a few."

"Me too," I said.

Seth was stirring something that smelled terrific. I went up the creek and filtered tea water.

"I guess we won't have to worry about the record books," I said, as I returned to the fire.

As the nineteenth century drew to a close, the mountainous interior of the Olympic Peninsula was the largest unexplored area of wilderness left in the lower 48 states. On a clear day, the snowcapped ramparts of the eastern Olympics seemed almost within the grasp of bustling 1880s Seattle. Yet more than a century after Spanish explorer Juan Perez first saw Mount Olympus from a three-masted ship, the Olympics remained cloaked in mystery. Maps of the era show a few small waterfront villages and a vast empty interior. "Terra Incognita" and "Unnamed and Unknown" were the words used to describe the region. The Olympics were truly, as historian Murray Morgan described them in his book of the same name, *The Last Wilderness.*

Then in 1885, Lt. Joseph P. O'Neil, a young Notre Dame graduate stationed near present-day Port Townsend, persuaded his superiors to authorize an expedition into the Olympics. Using Port Angeles as a staging area, O'Neil and his men laboriously climbed the steep north face of the mountains. The view from the summit was a surprise. Rather than the vast savannah or the huge inland sea promised by legends—and instead of a classic mountain divide like the Cascades or Rockies—the Olympic Mountains sprawled chaotically for as far as the eye could see. O'Neil's report described a virtual labyrinth of snowcapped peaks "reaching in wild broken confusion" above densely-timbered river valleys.

Four years later, in response to a challenge by the *Seattle Press* newspaper, James Christie and a rag-tag group of adventurers headed up the Elwha River Valley in midwinter. The following spring, after suffering through one of the most severe winters on record, Christie and his men emerged from the mountains at Lake Quinault, becoming the first whites to cross the Olympics. Later that year, Lt. O'Neil returned to the Olympics as commander of the Olympic Mountain Expedition, the first large scale military and scientific exploration of the interior Olympics. For more than four months, O'Neil and his men blazed trails, gathered flora and fauna and explored the southern and southeastern Olympics.

All of these parties encountered an abundance of game in the backcountry, and they supplemented their beans and bacon with elk and grouse, bear and venison. They also took advantage of the fish in the larger mountain streams. In Robert L. Wood's excellent book, *Across the Olympic Mountains—The Press Expedition, 1889-90,* he quotes a passage from Christie's diary that describes fishing in Geyser Valley on the upper Elwha: "Then followed one-half-hour of as fine fishing as any I ever enjoyed... carrying to camp fourteen splendid trout; weight about forty pounds; no mean basket from any water." In his history on the O'Neil expedition, *Men, Mules and Mountains—Lieutenant O'Neil's Olympic Expedition,* Wood similarly cites a passage from Pvt. Harry Fisher's journal that chronicles an evening's fishing on the upper reaches of the North Fork of the Skokomish: "There seemed to be but one size of trout. . . every one was the picture of the first caught, weighing 2 1/2#." A month later and many miles upstream, Fisher wrote, "and the catch numbered thirty good-sized brook trout."

Yet when O'Neil's men tried their flies and spoons on the mountain lakes of the southeastern Olympics, they invariably came away empty-handed. "Passing by Hearts Lake, which we named from its shape, we examined it for fish but found none," Fisher wrote, when he and another expedition member explored the subalpine and alpine lakes at the headwaters of the Duckabush and Dosewallips rivers. On the opposite corner of the Olympics, the crystal blue tarns that West End pioneer Chris Morganroth discovered in "The Basin of Seven Lakes" two years later were also barren of trout.

Some of the explorers believed the lakes were too cold for trout. Others thought the fish couldn't survive beneath the ice and snow that cover backcountry lakes for much of the year. Actually, the explanation was even simpler: The fish couldn't get up to them. You see, virtually all of the high-elevation lakes in the Olympic backcountry are located above impassable waterfalls or logjams. So despite the irrepressible colonizing instincts of the cutthroat, rainbow trout and Dolly Varden that teemed in its lowland lakes and mountain streams, the stillwaters of the high altitude Olympics remained fishless.

It didn't take long for this situation to be rectified. "Of the Eastern Brook trout, 85,000 were planted in the upper Soleduck and in Deer Lake at the head of Canyon Creek, a tributary to the Soleduck this past summer," Webster wrote in *Fishing in the Olympics*. And Morganroth reported that the Forest Service and Game Commission stocked four of the lakes in Seven Lakes Basin around 1924. By the beginning of World War II, trout could be found in nearly every accessible high-country lake. Anglers energetic enough to tramp into the high country often enjoyed a skillet full of firm-bodied, high-altitude trout for their dinner.

Because of quirks of geology, two areas of the Olympic Mountains contain a disproportionate number of productive mountain lakes. Seven Lakes Basin, the cluster of tarns that Chris Morganroth discovered at the head of the Sol Duc River, actually contains a dozen lakes. Sprawling more than 60 miles across the northern and eastern Olympics, the boomerang-shaped ridge of basalt known as the Crescent Formation is virtually sprinkled with high-country lakes. Lakes in both of these areas support self-sustaining populations of trout, predominately brook and rainbow, and they occasionally turn out fish that push the 20-inch mark.

According to National Park Service geologist Rowland Tabor, Seven Lakes Basin is unique among the high country areas in the western Olympics because its sandstone has resisted erosion. This has allowed the lakes in the basin to persist long after similar lakes filled with silt and were converted to meadows. Tabor suggests that the glaciers along the basin's north wall didn't leave the upper Sol Duc until after areas with southern and western exposures, which means that the basin is geologically "newer" and has had less time to be altered by the elements.

To understand the Crescent Formation, it is important to know what happened after the building blocks of the Olympics rose from the sea. Basically, the basalt of the seamounts was pushed into a narrow band along the north and east corner of the uplift, while the remainder of the dome was composed of sandstone and shale. Over many thousands of years, the combined forces of wind and rain, rivers and glaciation carved deeply into the relatively soft sedimentary rock of the western Olympics. Today, these areas are characterized by broad, terraced river valleys that stretch many miles from the high country to the sea. On the north and east sides of the Olympics, however, the Crescent Formation was much more resistant to the elements. The peaks rise sharply from the lowlands here, and the valleys are narrow and steep, drained by cataract-strewn, whitewater rivers. At the head of these rivers, amid the heather meadows and wildflowers, fishermen find gem-like mountain lakes.

As you might expect, there have been some changes in the Olympic backcountry since the days of O'Neil and Christie. For one thing, there are now more than 800 miles of maintained trail in Olympic National Park and the adjacent Buckhorn, Brothers, Mount Skokomish, Wonder Mountain and Colonel Bob Wilderness areas. Today llamas are much more common in the backcountry than horses, let alone the mules that the explorers preferred. In an attempt to preserve the delicate subalpine and alpine ecosystems, fires are now prohibited in the high country. And although the backcountry lakes seem completely wild, the National Park Service closely monitors the lakes in the park, and U.S. Forest Service fisheries biologist Michael Donald and his team conduct in-depth surveys of all Wilderness Area lakes and make stocking recommendations to the WDFW.

In the most profound ways, however, little has changed in the high country in the last century. Unlike other Western mountain ranges, which are bisected by highways and decorated with ski lodges, the backcountry of the Olympic Mountains is still accessible only to those vigorous enough to hoist a backpack. Indeed, in all of the park's 900,000 acres and the 120,000 acres within the Wilderness Areas, there is not a single mountain lake that can be reached by car. Moreover, fishermen that hike on weekdays and choose lakes beyond the reach of day hikers often have a cirque all to themselves. Backpacking fishermen in the Olympic Mountains can still enjoy experiences that are as dramatic and memorable as anything they can imagine.

About five years ago, for example, I hiked seven miles into a small brook-trout lake in the northeast corner of the national park. Located on the opposite side of the talus ridge that rises above the lake Seth and I fished, this lake enjoys one of the most beautiful settings in the Olympics. Rugged, snowcapped peaks tower more than 2,000 feet above its shoreline. Blacktail deer browse among lupine and bog gentian.

A chironomid hatch boiled off the lake as I pulled on my waders and laced up my shoes. Fish were rising everywhere. In my experience, mountain trout—even brook trout, which are disdained in some quarters as witless naïfs, but whom I suspect actually possess a tad more guile than most cutthroat often become extremely pattern conscious when a lake is glassy smooth. Fortunately, the late afternoon thermals that are a daily occurrence in the mountains during hot weather riffled the lake surface. I tied on a Griffith's Gnat, a fly I have had success with under similar conditions.

It was fast and furious. I caught three brook trout in less than 10 minutes. The biggest was probably 10 inches, the smallest two inches shorter. But they were all fat, lively—and staggeringly beautiful. Although it was mid-July, they all wore the vivid orange markings of their spawning dress. The deep black of their backs set off the crimson spots and blue halos on their flanks.

That night the bottomless darkness of the backcountry sky pulsed with stars. It was raining the next morning when I crawled from the tent, however, a chilling, high-country rain. Thick clouds hung over the nearby peaks. I had to be back in town that afternoon, so I broke camp quickly. I ate a handful of granola and cheese, then headed down the valley.

As you leave the swampy, willow-choked lowlands below the lake, the trail climbs sharply over a rocky spur. I worked up a sweat despite the rain and paused near the top of the trail to rest. The paintbrush and lupine in an old avalanche chute seemed especially vivid in the gray morning air. I was vaguely aware of a high-pitched sound nearby, but I didn't pay any attention to it. I remember thinking absently: marmot.

Suddenly, the sound became much louder and more intense. Turning away from the flowers, I faced a full-grown cougar. It sat on its haunches 15 feet down the trail. It didn't look happy. When our gazes met, it tilted its black-muzzled face and screamed. Then it raked the air with its left paw. Reacting completely on instinct, I shook my rod tube at the cougar. "Get out of here," I said.

The cat sliced at the air again with its paw. Then we both stared at each other. I remember noticing how cold its eyes looked. Somehow they seemed much wilder, more unfathomable, than the elk and deer and coyotes—even bears—I regularly encountered in the backcountry.

"Go on," I shouted, waving the rod tube again. "Get out of here."

But it didn't respond. I was a little worried. But then it stood up and in one sinuous motion bounded down the trail. Its tawny coat and long tail were the last things I saw as it disappeared around a basalt outcrop.

I just stood there for a moment, muttering things like "Jesus Christ" and "Man, oh man." Then a riot of conflicting thoughts tumbled across my mind. "Did that really happen?" I remember thinking. "God, I can't wait to tell someone." And, finally, sinkingly "It ran down trail—the way I have to go to get out of here."

I reached into my jeans for my pocket knife. My hands were shaking wildly, like they do after a fistfight, and it took several tries to retrieve the knife. I knew the old Buck knife that I used to clean small trout and slice cheese was an absurd weapon against a cougar. And, besides, I didn't think I would see it again. But I had to walk out the same way it had gone, and it made me feel a little safer.

I waited about five minutes, then headed down the trail. For the first 10 or 15 minutes, as I walked beneath rocky outcrops, I whistled and sang and carried my knife open. I felt stupid, but I was more than six miles from my car and I hadn't seen another human being since I broke camp that morning.

After I left the spur and came out onto the meadow and side hills, I felt safer. I put the knife away and stopped making noise. I still kept a sharp lookout on the trail behind me. But I had already begun the mysterious process that transforms experience into memory.

Hiking fishermen may choose from 800 miles of trails in Olympic National Park and five adjacent wilderness areas.

Chapter 10

The Crook

That Stole the Brook

The first notion that crossed my mind when I woke was, "My car is 15 miles away, back at the Elwha River Trailhead, and I don't have to head back for two more days." Then I remembered that the three noisily competitive Chamber of Commerce types had packed up their $35,000 worth of high-tech fly fishing and backpacking gear the afternoon before and headed back toward Whiskey Bend. When I stuck my head outside the tent, the glowering clouds and drizzle of the day before had been replaced by a flawless Boca Chica Key blue. That tied a nice ribbon around my sense of well-being.

I pulled on my hiking shorts and boots and crawled out of the tent. Now that the swells had gone, the riverside flat was as empty and quiet as a fairground on the morning after the circus leaves town. I took a deep breath of the moist river bottom air and stared up at the peaks between Mount Dana and Mount Wilder. The sun hadn't climbed above the ridge to the east, and it was cold in the shade. I was tempted to crawl back into my sleeping bag for another hour.

Instead, I slipped into my rag sweater and old North Face down vest. I retrieved the kindling I had stored in the tent to keep dry and my paperback John D. McDonald mystery. I ripped out the six pages I had read the night before and balled them up, a fire-starting trick I had learned from Keith McCafferty, *Field & Stream's* excellent writer. After I had a nice, crackling tea fire going, I carried my small cook kit sauce pan down to the river. I filled it with numbingly cold river water and propped it on the fire.

Rising deep in the mountainous interior of Olympic National Park, a few miles from the headwaters of the Hoh and Queets, the Elwha River is the fourth largest river on the peninsula. On its 45-mile journey from the tangle of peaks and snowfields south of Mount Olympus to tidewater on the Strait of Juan de Fuca, the Elwha drains 321 square miles of the north central Olympics. The Elwha River Trail, which follows the path blazed by the Press Expedition, parallels the upper river through 25 miles of wilderness to Low Divide, the pass between the Elwha and North Fork of the Quinault watersheds. Between midsummer and the close of the season at the end of October, the backcountry Elwha between Elkhorn Camp and Buckinghorse Creek offers the best fly fishing for resident trout on the Olympic Peninsula.

My fly rod was propped against a tree near the tent. I carried it down to the broken, boulder-strewn pocket water in front of my camp. I rock-hopped out onto a large, flat-topped boulder without getting too wet, then stretched my tippet and tested the knot on my big, black stonefly nymph. The night before, I had discovered that a quartered upstream cast with my 10-foot sink tip and a 3-foot leader gave me about 10 feet of bottom bouncing before the current swung the fly around downstream. I hadn't taken any fish—all my fish so far had come fishing caddis patterns—but I was certain I would sooner or later.

It turned out to be sooner, on the fly's second drift, as a matter of fact. The fly drifted about six feet, then I felt that vague, "different" sensation that often telegraphs the take of a fish. I stretched the slack in my left hand and quickly jerked back with the rod. A fish splashed wildly across the surface. It was a 14-inch rainbow, thick-bodied, with the small head and dazzling crimson strip common to Elwha backcountry rainbows. It was solidly hooked, and after a few minutes I worked it up to the rock. I released it.

I had the whole day to fish, so I went back to camp, made tea and ate a handful of granola, half of a bagel and a chunk of cheese. The sun had crawled over the ridge-line, filling the river bottom with puddles of light. Leaning back against the trunk of a fir tree, I made notes for an article that was due the following week.

After an hour or so, I began to nod off under the warm sun. I put the notebook away, exchanged my down vest for my fly vest and walked downstream. A quarter mile or so below camp, the river forked around a small, apostrophe-shaped island. The flow of water around the outside curve of the island was broken and fast, typical stonefly water. But the soft green water on the inside hook of the apostrophe was smooth, slow and deep. Trout rose rhythmically to hatching insects.

Although they were too far away to distinguish anatomical details, I could tell from their silhouettes and the way they flew they were mayflies. Unfortunately, a bankside willow thicket and the deep water prevented me from getting close enough to identify them. But they seemed vaguely yellowish in the bright midday sun. And since it was the right time of year and type of water, I figured they were probably Pale Morning Duns.

Now, I am normally an unreconstructed member of the impressionist school of fly fishermen—that is, I tend to think knowing where the fish are and how to present a fly to them is more important than a scrupulously representative fly pattern. In this regard, I am in complete agreement with E.B. Webster. "It may be true that in the Eastern states, and on some of the most-fished streams of the West the trout are very particular, necessitating a large assortment of flies to match their whims," he wrote in *Fishing in the Olympics*. "But here in the Olympics one will not go far wrong if his kit be limited to a piece of line and two or three brown hackles. . ." Similarly, I take 90 percent of my backcountry trout on Adams', Elk Hair Caddis, Gold Ribbed Hare's Ears and stonefly nymphs.

However, in exchange for directions to a summer-run hole on the Queets, a friend of mine had recently presented me with three dozen flies of my own choosing. I had asked for a half dozen soft hackle patterns, specifically the March Brown Spiders discussed in Dave Hughes' *Western Streamside Guide*. In anticipation of the Elwha's abundant caddis, I had also requested a selection of Gary LaFontaine's Deep Sparkle Pupa, Emergent Sparkle Pupa and Dancing Caddis. I had just reread Cuacci and Nastasi's *Mayflies* and, on a whim, asked for a dozen olive/yellow comparadun patterns.

So I was elated when I saw the mayflies. There aren't many chances to fish mayfly-inspired patterns on Olympic Peninsula rivers. But I had stumbled onto a modest hatch miles from anywhere, completely surrounded by stonefly and caddis water. And for once I was actually prepared.

I snipped the heavy stonefly nymph off my tippet and built a 12-foot leader. Because of the deep slow water and bankside vegetation, the only way to present the fly was from directly upstream. It wasn't a difficult cast, only about 35 feet, but I don't get a lot of chances to sight fish and I was tentative on my first two casts. The fly landed well short of the fish. I laid the fly down just a few feet above the trout on the next few casts, and it drifted into their feeding lanes without drag. The trout ignored the fly.

By now, I was in something of a state. As I said, I'm not in the habit of making delicate presentations to surface-feeding trout anymore. I had this absolute certainty that at any moment I would shank a cast and my leader would land in a tangle right on top of the fish. But I was also extremely excited about having an opportunity to actually match a hatch. I stood there for a moment, not knowing what to do next.

Finally, it occurred to me to change flies. I was still pretty sure that the mayflies were Pale Morning Duns. But I remembered that my friend had tied me two sizes of the comparaduns, 16s and 18s. For no particular reason, I had tied on the larger fly. I replaced it with the 18.

After stripping the appropriate amount of line, I took three deep breaths, then cast. The line turned over perfectly and the fly settled lightly on the water five feet above the fish. Bent over at the waist like a home plate umpire, I fed line through my index finger. There was a swirl as the fly drifted into the feeding lane, then I saw the back of a fish.

Swinging back with the rod, I felt the immensely satisfying resistance of a fish. At the prick of the barb, the trout jumped twice, shattering the placid green water. It was a little smaller than the one I had caught earlier, maybe a foot long. But it fought like a miniature steelhead, pulling line off my small Pflueger and leaping repeatedly. It took twice as long to land as most fish its size.

I released it, then headed back toward camp. On my way upstream, I noticed caddisflies hovering above a sunny riffle. It occurred to me that if I took a trout on a caddis pattern I would have succeeded in landing an Elwha fish on each of the three classic subaquatic insects—stoneflies, mayflies and caddis—in one day. On a place like the Olympic Peninsula, where hatch matching is not a significant part of the fly fishing experience, this "Elwha Grand Slam" had a definite appeal.

Although the backcountry Elwha is known primarily as caddis water, I had to work harder with my Trichoptera patterns than with either the stonefly nymph or the comparadun. Neither the soft hackle nor the pupal or emerger patterns produced so much as a tickle. Finally, I noticed that the fish had begun to hit insects on the surface. I tied on a Dancing Caddis. I cast directly downstream, then skittered the fly upstream on a tight line for six feet. I let it drift back downstream. A fish smacked the fly just as I prepared to lift the line off the water and cast again.

It was nearly identical to the last trout, a foot-long wild Elwha rainbow. I brought it

to hand as quickly as possible, then released it. As I waded to shore, I looked at my watch. It was a few minutes before noon.

On the wall behind my writing desk, there is a photograph of a young woman standing by a river. I would guess the woman is about 20 years old. Slender and fetching in a field of wildflowers, she smiles shyly into the camera. She is wearing a skirt and lace-up boots. In her right hand she holds a fly rod. She holds a fish in her left hand.

The woman in the photo is Elinor Chittenden. The river is the Elwha. Taken by Asahel Curtis, brother of the renowned photographer of American Indians, Samuel Sheriff Curtis, the photo is one of a series taken on a 1907 expedition into the Elwha backcountry by the Mountaineers, a Seattle outdoor organization. The fish, which stretches from just below Miss Chittendon's shoulder to well below her knees, is a wild summer-run steelhead. The photo was taken within sight of timberline and glaciers, several miles upstream of the campsite where I took my "Elwha Grand Slam."

The Elwha was one of the most productive anadromous fish systems in the Northwest when the Mountaineers pushed into the Olympic backcountry. In addition to summer steelhead like Elinor Chittendon's, winter steelhead, sea-run cutthroat and migratory Dolly Varden swam deep into the Elwha backcountry. Chum salmon spawned in the side channels, sockeye swam up an Elwha tributary to Lake Sutherland and coho flashed into the tributaries. Every other year, a run of pink salmon swarmed into the river during late summer, sometimes 150,000 strong. Most impressive of all, the Elwha's legendary "tyee" Chinook reached weights of 100 pounds and the length of a man's span.

Unfortunately, less than five years later Thomas Aldwell, a Canadian-born promoter with financing from a group of Chicago venture capitalists, built a hydroelectric dam on the Elwha less than five miles from the river mouth. Although in clear violation of an 1890 Washington law that prevented dams that blocked access to streams where "food fish are wont to ascend" the dam had no fish passage facilities. Instantly, more than 70 miles of mainstem river and spawning tributaries, 93 percent of the watershed, was inaccessible to migratory fish. Within a spawning cycle, the river above the dams was as barren of salmon as a hay mound, while the upstream trout and char were transformed into "resident" populations. Biologists estimate that dams reduced the river's salmonid population by 75 percent.

A second dam was built at Glines Canyon at river-mile 13 in 1926. This divided the river into three sections, with three entirely different fisheries. The anadromous fish were confined to the 4.9 miles below the Elwha dam. Paralleled by a road, the middle section of the river was now essentially a rainbow trout stream. Above Glines Canyon Dam, the river climbed for more than 30 miles through roadless wilderness, which has been protected within the borders of Olympic National Park since 1938.

In the years after the dams, the fishing remained good. "Here he grows to truly immense size, specimens eighteen and twenty inches in length being, if not very common, at least sufficiently so that one would never think of packing them very far for the pleasure of exhibiting them to his friends," Webster wrote of the "rainbows" above the dams. And as late as the 1950s fall Chinook in the 50-pound range still returned to the river from time to time. The current Washington record Chinook salmon is a 70-pound, 8-ounce Elwha fish that Chet Gausta took off Sekiu on September 6, 1964.

But there were problems. Crowding all of the surviving migratory fish into less than 10 percent of the watershed increased stress and encouraged the spread of disease. The dams also blocked the downstream flow of sand, gravel and woody debris that replenish spawning grounds and provide habitat for juvenile fish and aquatic insects. Gradually, decade by decade, the salmon and trout populations declined. Even the resident rainbows of the middle river suffered, the victims of easy access and deteriorating habitat.

In response to declining runs, the Washington Department of Fisheries began to enhance Elwha fall Chinook in 1930. By 1965, the state was also planting steelhead and coho in the lower river. As a result of mitigation agreement with the dam owners, the WDF opened a spawning channel on the Elwha in 1973. The Lower Elwha Band of the S'Klallam Tribe, whose economy had suffered as a result of declining salmon runs, began to release salmon and steelhead from their own hatchery four years later.

The hundreds of thousands of fish released by the state and tribe created a "put and take" fishery during the late 1970s and early 1980s. "I lived at the mouth of the Elwha for nine years in the 70s," West End fly fishing guide J. D. Love recalls. "One December I caught 25 steelhead." But the hatchery fish only masked the fact that the Elwha was teetering on the verge of collapse as a producer of wild fish.

During the late 1970s and 1980s, a number of agencies and organizations began to grapple with the problem of getting migratory fish above the dams. The Department of the Interior, the Washington Department of Fish and Wildlife, the S'Klallam Tribe, Trout Unlimited and a host of environmental organizations were granted intervenor status in the dam owner's attempts to license the dams with the Federal Energy Regulatory Commission. In addition, the U.S. Fish and Wildlife Service conducted experiments that showed that modest numbers of juvenile salmon and steelhead could survive downstream passage over the dam. But there were still no passage facilities for adult fish on the Elwha dams and no consensus on whether any amount of technological tinkering would ever restore fish to the upper river. By the end of the decade, a growing number of organizations and individuals had begun to call for dam removal.

Finally, in an attempt to prevent further litigation and to bypass the tortuous FERC process, Washington Senator Brock Adams and New Jersey Senator Bill Bradley drafted a legislative solution in early 1991. The Elwha River Ecosystem and Fisheries Restoration Act ordered the Secretary of the Interior to determine whether dam removal was necessary for fisheries and ecosystem restoration and, if so, to develop a plan for dam removal. It also stipulated that the federal government would purchase the dams for $29.5 million and would provide discount BPA power for the Port Angeles mill that used the dams' electricity. Widely heralded as something of a miracle, the Elwha Act met the approval of the tribes, the agencies, the sporting and environmental communities and the dam owners. Congress passed the bill in the summer of 1992, and President Bush signed it into law a few weeks before the 1992 presidential election.

It was a heady time. Local anglers and the S'Klallam Tribe had dreamed of seeing fish in the upper river since the first year of dam operation. But what had once seemed fantastic—the removal of the dams—now seemed not only possible but likely. Moreover, with more than 80 percent of the river in pristine condition, there was consensus among biologists that the Elwha possessed the greatest potential for fish restoration of any river in the Northwest.

But the celebration didn't last long. No sooner had the bill been signed than it became apparent that the 1990s were perhaps the least favorable time for Elwha River restoration, especially dam removal, than any decade since Aldwell and cronies dammed the river. To begin with, the federal budget deficit resulted in a tightening and much closer examination of all expenditures. It was also fashionable to question whether the federal government was capable of successfully completing any complex large-scale project. The political climate in the country had also shifted sharply to the right, especially in the West, where a deep

suspicion, if not outright hostility, toward government agencies was common.

Still, the Elwha Act was law, and the DOI pursued its mandate. In early 1994 it released "The Elwha Report," which concluded: "The removal of the Elwha and Glines Canyon dams is the only alternative that would result in the 'full restoration of the Elwha River ecosystem and native anadromous fisheries.'" Several months later, it reported to Congress that there was a very good chance that nine out of 10 of the runs could be restored with dam removal. Citing an economic analysis by an independent consultant, the DOI also claimed that dam decommissioning would provide $90.4 million in gross income to workers in the region and would generate an additional $21.1 for Clallam County businesses.

Speaking at the Wild Trout V Conference in Denver, Secretary of the Interior Bruce Babbitt told the assembled fish managers and biologists that he wanted to "be the first Secretary of the Interior to blow up a dam." When pressed by reporters about what dam he was talking about, Babbitt explained that he meant the dams on the Elwha.

That was not what Washington Senator Slade Gorton wanted to hear. A supporter of the Elwha Act when Manuel Lujan, the most supine and inept Secretary of the Interior in this century, controlled the fate of the dams, Gorton became a vocal opponent of dam removal after Babbitt took over at Interior. Gorton now proposed a two-year funding deadline for Elwha restoration. If Congress failed to appropriate the money for the project within that time, Gorton wanted to relicense the dams for 20 years and spend $25 million on Olympic Peninsula salmon enhancement.

To most observers, Gorton's proposals seemed like nothing more than a back-handed attempt to block dam removal. "Completing the environmental impact statements and preparing the paperwork for removing the Elwha dams alone will take about two years," Trout Unlimited government affairs director Steve Moyer told Alison M. Rice in the winter 1995 issue of *Trout.* "Gorton's bill undercuts the work of a broad coalition who share a vision of returning these runs to the Elwha."

If Gorton wanted to undercut dam removal efforts, the 1994 off-year elections gave him a perfect opportunity. Indeed, when Republicans took control of the 104th Congress in January of 1995, Gorton became the chairman of the Senate Appropriations subcommittee on the Interior. Gorton now controlled not only the purse strings for Elwha restoration but for the entire Department of the Interior. And although his efforts to reopen old growth forest to unregulated logging and to repeal the Endangered Species Act kept him busy, Gorton took the time to make his views on the Elwha known.

"From both a policy perspective and as a matter of fiscal policy, my views are crystal clear on the subject of dam removal: I do not support it," Gorton said in a statement released the day before the release of the final Elwha Restoration Environmental Impact Statement.

The EIS, as expected, once again called for dam removal. "Only the removal of both dams can restore the Elwha River and its fisheries," Olympic National Park Superintendent Dave Morris told the *Peninsula Daily News* upon its release. The report estimated the cost of restoration at between $75 and $101 million dollars over a 20 year period, but claimed a free-flowing river would bring in $133 million in recreation and tourism over the long haul. More than 85 percent of the comment letters published in the EIS were in favor of dam removal. As had been the case on "The Elwha Report" and the draft EIS, the Elinor Chittenden photo graced the inside of the report.

Gorton countered with an announcement that the "community" should come up with a restoration project without dam removal within one year. Otherwise, he

warned, Congress would impose its own solution. Gorton didn't specify what he meant by "community."

A short time later, a Port Angeles group, Rescue Elwha Area Lakes, announced it had hired Robert Crittenden, the *Salmon at Risk* author, to develop a restoration plan for the Elwha. Long-time opponents of dam removal, REAL maintained that getting fish above the dams was simply a matter of trapping them in the lower river, then hauling them around the dams in trucks. REAL cited the sockeye run on the Baker River, a Skagit River tributary with two hydroelectric dams, as proof that salmon and dams could coexist.

Unfortunately, not one objective fisheries biologist that had studied the Elwha believed that REAL's ideas would ever result in a self-sustaining run of salmon or trout. The trap and haul technique proposed by REAL, for example, guaranteed that returning adult fish would suffer unacceptably high levels of stress and mortality. The REAL plan also failed to address the severely degraded spawning and nursery habitat on the middle and lower river. In addition, Crittenden was on record as having written "as it is expected that under most conditions there will be some weak stocks, fishing should not be curtailed, nor the structure of the fishery altered to preserve or enhance these stocks." As for the Baker River, after decades of just the sort of mechanistic enhancement that REAL proposed for the Elwha, there were neither sport nor tribal fisheries for any species on the river and its sockeye had recently been described as a "critical" stock in the state and tribes Salmon and Steelhead Stock Inventory.

About the only thing the REAL plan promised to accomplish was to satisfy Senator Gorton's demand that a local group devise a plan in which the dams stayed in place. Perhaps that was its only intent. REAL's response to the draft Elwha EIS, for example, makes many of the same arguments as the letter submitted jointly by the North Olympic Homebuilders' Association and the Building Industry Association of Washington. The Homebuilders' letter was prepared by James Johnson, an Olympia attorney with ties to Senator Gorton.

Meanwhile, Elwha anadromous fish continued their free fall toward oblivion. A paper published by Willa Nehlson, Jack Williams and James Lichatowich in the journal of American Fisheries Society in the early 1990s characterized native Elwha coho as "at high risk of extinction" and claimed that Elwha chum may already be extinct. Only four pink salmon returned to the Elwha in 1993, down from historic highs of upwards of 100,000 fish. And despite a summer-long salmon closure in the Strait of Juan de Fuca, less than half the anticipated number of fall Chinook returned to the river in 1995 and many of these fish were diseased.

Not surprisingly, the people that had worked on Elwha restoration for years viewed this unfolding debacle with mounting dismay. More than half a century ago, Roderick Haig-Brown wrote prophetically about dams and anadromous fish: "A solution to the problems of high dams on salmon streams is nowhere in sight. It may not be impossible—few things are. But it will never be found by mechanical means, by gadgets and guesswork and grandiose schemes to fool the public and quieten the consciences of the money makers. It will be found, if anywhere at all, in the fish themselves." Nonetheless, the shelves at the University of Washington School of Fisheries library groan under the weight of these schemes. And despite the glaring, front page collapse of Columbia and Snake river fish runs—and the earlier, quieter extinction of more than 100 major West Coast stocks of anadromous fish—there were still people who claimed that a gauntlet of fish ladders, truck transport and hatchery dependence would serve Elwha fish better than a free-flowing river.

It was in this context that I paid a visit to Jeff Bohman, the Elwha River Restoration Coordinator for the S'Klallam

Tribe. I had met Jeff at a Friends of the Elwha meeting earlier in the year and had been impressed by his grasp of both the details of Elwha restoration and its larger significance. I had also enjoyed watching him cow the choleric pensioners, right wing cranks and Indian haters that haunt all public meetings on the Olympic Peninsula these days.

We talked in his office at the Elwha Tribal Center on the reservation. A bulletin board in the lobby announced Head Start schedules, S'Klallam language classes and firewood for sale. Phones rang constantly, but the office didn't have the nail-biting angst common to business and government offices.

Jeff and I chatted for a while about the brilliant fall weather. Then I asked him the question I had thought about on the drive from Port Townsend to Port Angeles.

"What do you think restoring the Elwha would mean to residents of the north Olympic Peninsula?"

Jeff paused, as he framed his thoughts. "It would be in two different ways," he finally said. "As a representative of the Native American community, it is very apparent to me how organically these people did live and could live again with the river. The Elwha and its fish have been the tribe's central unifying foundation for centuries. It is hard to imagine a tribe anywhere else that has it so within its grasp to reclaim the substantial essence of whom they are.

"For the rest of us, the Elwha could become the mother river for the entire north Olympic Peninsula. It is the largest river on the strait. It's the most protected. It had all of the salmon species, substantial numbers of them. Restoring the river would also bring back the shellfish at the mouth and stop the erosion on Ediz Hook. And in an area that has a desperate need for jobs, the restoration would create 500 jobs and bring more than $4 million a year into the community."

My next question was an attempt to

understand something that had bothered me ever since opposition to dam removal began.

"One of the main arguments the opponents of dam removal make is that it won't restore the fishery," I said. "They say, 'The Dungeness doesn't have any dams and its salmon are gone too.' But these people truly don't seem to comprehend that the Elwha is different, that more than 80 percent of it is in the same condition as before white people came to the peninsula. They don't seem to understand that this is an unique opportunity."

Jeff nodded. "The Elwha has a nearly pristine watershed. It doesn't have the irrigation demands that the Dungeness does. The land is in excellent condition. We don't have any of the problems on the Elwha that plague other rivers. Restoring the Elwha, really, isn't that big a deal. Some money needs to be spent and some demolition work done, then the river will take care of itself."

I would liked to have talked to Jeff longer, but I had another interview scheduled later that afternoon. We shook hands and agreed to keep in touch. I carried my notes to my truck and slowly drove through the reservation. Looking south, up the Elwha Valley, I could see fresh snow on Mount Carrie, the glacier-flanked mountain that guards the entrance to the Elwha backcountry. The camp where I took my "Elwha Grand Slam" was a dozen miles beyond the mountain. Elinor Chittenden caught her steelhead even further upriver, nearly 40 miles from the mouth.

I stopped by the sign announcing Elwha Bingo. Suddenly, I remembered a quatrain I had read in the Washington Department of Fisheries' publication a few years earlier:

"The law locks up that man that
takes the salmon from the brook;
but lets loose the larger crook that
from the salmon steals the brook."

Chapter 11

Estuaries

I leaned forward with the oars, then drew them back through the heavy gray water. Across the two-mile expanse of Dungeness Bay, the seagulls wheeling above a herring ball looked tiny and delicate, like a spinner fall of mayflies. Beyond them, the immaculate white tower of the New Dungeness Lighthouse rose above the flat enclosing arm of Dungeness Spit. To the east, the skeletal pilings of an abandoned grain trestle reached a half mile into the bay.

If I had been in a typical Puget Sound salmon fishing boat, I might have screeched over to the bird works. I might have dipped a bucket of herring from the roiling, iridescent hummock of baitfish. Then I could have raced out to the eddy at the end of the spit and tried to mooch a late-returning Chinook salmon.

But I didn't own one of those gleaming, testosterone bombs. No, my boat was a 12-foot wooden skiff I had bought at the Northwest School of Wooden Boatbuilding for $400. And instead of a heavy rod and star drag reel, there was an 8-weight fly rod and a Pflueger Medalist, model 1498, lying in the bottom of the boat. I wasn't after kings, as Chinook salmon are referred to in Washington. I was fishing for coho, the fly fisherman's salmon.

It was late October. Four days earlier, I had waded the shoreline near the mouth of the Dungeness River, casting small shrimp patterns and Lefty's Deceivers for cutthroat. I didn't turn a fish. But as I neared the river mouth, I began to see salmon, coho salmon. Rolling and porpoising, they hung along the edge of the deep water off the river delta. Unfortunately, they were well beyond the reach of my wading and casting.

The sight of all of those salmon was more than I could resist. On my next day off, I launched my boat at the ramp near the

Dungeness Oyster House. It wasn't a long row, less than a mile. But there was a fairly stiff breeze out of the east and the flat bottom of the skiff didn't take the waves very well. In fact, rowing through the small chop was similar to the trotting gait of some horses, not my favorite sensation.

It was wonderful being on the bay, though. Indeed, autumn on Dungeness Bay—or any bay or river delta, for that matter—is a feast for the senses. The sound of geese and the smell of wood smoke fill the air. Tawny, timber-topped bluffs rise in the distance. Russet-colored sedges shimmy in the flooding tide. And the rhythmic action of rowing is soothing.

This was more than 10 years ago, when I was just starting to fly fish for salmon. I spent a lot of autumn days on estuaries back then, because I knew that once the salmon entered the river, snaggers would descend upon them like magpies on road kill. After that happened, my salmon fishing would be over for the year. From long experience, I knew that I could not enjoy myself while I was bristling with rage. But if I learned how to take salmon between the techno fishermen in deep water and the snaggers upstream, I would have a month or more of fishing in virtual solitude every autumn.

I eased up on the oars and stretched my back. Turning around to see how far I had come, I discovered that the river mouth was only about 50 yards away. Then, as I reached back to pick up the oars, I saw a fish roll in the general area of my fly. I dropped the oars and reached for the rod. I grabbed it with my right hand, intending to quickly strip the small shrimp pattern back in, then cast in the direction of the fish.

But there was resistance when I lifted the rod. When I jerked back harder, a chunky, chrome-bright fish thrashed on the surface, kicking up a rainbow of spray. Quickly switching the rod to my other hand, I remember thinking, "Jesus, it's hooked itself."

It raced away from the boat, getting into my backing in no time. At the end of its run, it jumped three times. Then it stopped briefly, almost as though it were puzzling over what to do next. I gained back a few yards of line before it took off again. This time it jumped twice.

By now, the boat had drifted into the shallows off the river mouth. The oar on the beach side of the boat, which I had failed to ship in the excitement of hooking the fish, hung up on the bottom. For a moment, the skiff teetered back and forth, pivoting on the oarlock. Then the wind caught the boat broadside and spun it around. Suddenly, I was facing the beach.

Swearing savagely, I shifted back toward the water. Fortunately, the salmon didn't take advantage of the situation. I quickly retrieved the slack I had dropped when the boat spun. Then I pumped gently on the rod and reeled. The fish thrashed and made short dashes, but I worked it steadily toward shore. The fight went on that way for a few more minutes. I was confident that the fish was well hooked, but I knew that I could lose it at any moment on a razor-sharp oyster bar or an abandoned crab pot.

Everything went smoothly, though, and presently I had a football-shaped salmon wallowing in the eel grass beside the boat. I snubbed the line down with my rod hand—a dangerous practice, I know, but I was alone—then raised the rod high. With my free hand, I grabbed my net and held it over the gunwhale above the fish's nose. I dipped the net and quickly scooped it over the fish.

As I lifted it from the water, a shaft of late afternoon light caught the fish. Its back flashed purple and green, like a mallard's head. Its flanks shimmered liquidly—rose, charcoal and silver.

By the summer solstice, most of the salmon that will spawn in Olympic Peninsula rivers during autumn have already bent their great migratory ellipses back in the direction of the Washington coast. Far to the north, Chinook salmon that have spent two, three or four years at sea now hug Vancouver Island's ragged western shoreline. Traveling well offshore, coho salmon work their way south from the Gulf of Alaska. Chum, sockeye and, in odd-numbered years, pink salmon—they all vector unerringly in on the Strait of Juan de Fuca and coastal rivers.

During the long days of early summer, the salmon move quickly, covering as much as 30 miles a day. At the absolute height of their vigor, the fish feed voraciously, somehow aware that they will need all of the energy they can store to successfully spawn. Then, as the sun slips back toward the south and the big tides of summer give way to the weaker tides of autumn, the salmon begin to marshall along the deltas and bays of Olympic Peninsula rivers.

Some are native to small coastal creeks, where only a few snag-choked tidal pools serve as buffers between the pounding of the North Pacific and the cedar-stained riffles upstream. But rivers like the Dungeness, Skokomish and Pysht bend their currents into vast bays, where ripening salmon gradually acclimate themselves to freshwater. And the rivers that tumble from the mile-high ramparts of the eastern Olympics tend to unravel over their deltas like the frayed ends of a rope. For the salmon of these rivers, the entire 60-mile length of Hood Canal—its clam flats and pocket coves, eel grass beds and oyster bars—is one large estuary.

Not all salmon return to the river during autumn, of course. Small numbers of Chinook trickle through the estuaries and enter the Queets and Hoh in early spring. Most of the peninsula's large river systems, especially those of glacial origin, also support modest runs of summer Chinook. Other unique, early-timed runs—the summer chum of Quilcene, Discovery and Sequim bays; the upriver pinks of the Dungeness and Graywolf rivers; the Sol Duc's "summer coho" and river-dwelling sockeye—also pass through tidewater before the first fall flight of teal. The Satsop's storied run of 20-pound silvers and the late chum of northern Hood Canal rivers, conversely, often do not spawn until well into January.

But Olympic Peninsula estuaries reach a crescendo of activity during autumn. Indeed, these fertile mixing grounds of fresh and saltwater virtually pulse with salmonids between September and the end of November. And anglers that have taken the time to chart the comings and goings of the fish and understand the behavior of salmon in brackish water can experience memorable sport.

In the years since my first Dungeness silver, I have spent many days wading and rowing along Olympic Peninsula beaches. I have also spent thousands of hours working next to the water—in hatcheries, as a field interviewer on a National Marine Fisheries Service project and as a journalist. I have had many opportunities to watch salmon close at hand in their near-shore environment. And I have taken my share of fish.

Yet I don't feel as though I know very much about fly fishing for salmon in estuaries. Let me put that another way: I know a few estuaries well; I know when the fish will be concentrated and where to position myself to intercept them; I know the workings of time, tide and light. But although different stocks of the same species of salmon tend to behave similarly during the sea-going and fresh water phases, it has been my experience that their behavior in estuaries is extremely site specific.

In other words, knowing how to catch, say, pink salmon off the Dosewallips doesn't necessarily transfer to knowing how to catch pinks in any other estuary. Similarly, knowing how to take Dosey pinks probably won't help you much when the chum return to the river three months later, either. And with more than 120 distinct runs of salmon returning to more than 40 Olympic rivers—well, I don't feel as though I know very much about estuary fishing.

Ironically, most of what I do know about Olympic Peninsula estuaries I learned while fishing for sea-run cutthroat. Cutthroat are available in saltwater over a much longer period of time than any species of salmon, typically from spring through at least early winter. They also feed more predictably than salmon and respond to the fly more readily. I spent a lot of time fishing cutts during my early days on the peninsula.

But I picked up salmon from time to time on those cutthroat trips—an occasional pink in July, a silver now and then, even a Chinook jack once. Looking back on those years, I think I actually caught more salmon while fishing for cutthroat than I did when I targeted salmon. That began to change eventually. I began to accumulate a body of knowledge about individual runs of salmon, about the conformation of the estuaries and river mouths. I learned bays that only produced on high tide, creek mouths that fished best on the ebb. I learned runs that preferred small shrimp patterns and others that only hit blue-green streamers.

I have never forgotten that nearly all of my early salmon were taken wading or rowing on estuaries for sea-runs. And when I prospect a new bay or river delta today, I approach it the same way I did Dungeness Bay all those years ago—casting or trolling near a river mouth in early autumn.

That's the way you learn estuaries—one bay, one run and one fish at a time.

Chapter 12

Dry Lines

I had spent the day on the Hoh, riffle hitching hair wings over my favorite summer steelhead lies. The river was in perfect shape for a floating line, but I didn't have a bump all day. It was dark by the time I drove back into the Hoh Rain Forest Campground. Fortunately, I had layed out a fire earlier. I cooked the jambalya I had bought from Tom Embrey, Port Townsend's wizard Cajun butcher, and ate it with crusty sourdough and a chunk of smoked gouda. I popped open a Labatt's.

By the time I finished eating, my last two pieces of firewood had burned down to gray-orange embers. I watched the heat pulse off the rectangular segments of wood for a long time, enjoying the warmth from the bed of coals beneath the logs. Then I carried my dishes down to the outdoor faucet near the campground restroom. I rinsed my sauce pan and plate, spoon and fork, and dumped the bottle in the trash. There was one other campfire in the A-Loop, the area of the campground the Park Service keeps open during late fall and winter. Everyone else was battened away behind the locked doors of their motor homes.

Walking back to my tent, I didn't bother with the flashlight. After moving away from the fire, I had discovered I could see quite well in the silvery light of the October moon. I put the cooking gear in the old, green Coleman cooler and set it inside the cab of the truck, where the burly, gangster-class rain forest raccoons wouldn't be tempted. Then on impulse I grabbed another beer and headed down to the sand bar between the campground and the river. I had read that steelhead and salmon often migrate at night, and I thought I might be able to catch a glimpse of one in the moonlight.

As I heeled down the slope to the bar, the cold off the river was palpable. I hopscotched across a little feeder creek, then picked my way toward the sleek, glacial hiss of the river. It was bright enough to see elk droppings and driftwood on the sand. Overhead, the frosty autumn sky shimmered with stars.

I couldn't see any fish, only the moon-flecked riffle and clay bank downstream. I sat on a snag and opened the beer. As I raised the bottle to my lips, I sensed motion. Startled, I scanned the darkness. I couldn't see anything at first. But then I began to pick out silhouettes—skinny legs, thick necks and high withers. It was elk. I had wandered into a herd that had bedded down on the sand bar.

I didn't move. The elk were facing me. I had apparently alarmed them enough to stand up, but not enough to actually run away. For a couple of minutes, they seemed anxious, like the leaves on an aspen that reveal the breeze before you can feel it. Then, one by one, they began to settle back down. I couldn't make out features, only the large shapes of cows and the smaller shapes of yearlings and calves.

I sat there for a long time. After a while, I could separate other sounds from the water over the rock roar of the river. I could hear the dry rasp of cottonwood leaves, the soughing of the Sitka spruce boughs. From time to time, I heard an elk stretch or shift. But there was also a resonant, rhythmic sound that I couldn't identify. Then it dawned on me that it, too, was the elk. I was actually close enough to hear them breathing!

I looked up at the three-dimensional fields of stars. Then I looked downstream to the pale puddles of light on the log jam at the base of the clay bank. I closed my eyes. I can hear elk breathing, I said to myself.

Finally, I stood up. I walked slowly back across the sand bar toward my tent. This time the elk didn't move. Grabbing at the brush, I pulled myself up the bank off the sand bar, then crossed the road. I turned back to look one last time, but the only thing I could see was the river.

All that was left of the elk the next morning were darker piles of scat and fresh depressions in the sand. I spent about an hour working a Bomber through the slicks and pocket water near the campground. I couldn't really concentrate, though. I think I instinctively wanted to savor my experience with the elk for a time, wanted to make sure I didn't dilute it with other activity.

I broke camp. I had planned to fish my way down the Upper Hoh Valley Road in the morning, hitting four or five spots along the way. And I would have stopped at the Westward Hoh and told Gene Owens about the elk, but the store hadn't opened yet. I drove straight to the highway.

I stopped in Forks and ate breakfast in the restaurant adjacent to the Pay and Save Shop-Rite. It was still well before noon when I finished eating. I walked across the street to Olympic Sporting Goods and talked to Bob Gooding about grouse hunting and river conditions. After a few minutes, a couple of out of town hunters came in wanting archery deer licenses, and I left. I got gas at the Gull station.

By now, I felt I had enough time to properly frame the experience of the night before. And since I didn't have to be back in Port Townsend until early evening, I decided to fish for a couple of hours. There wasn't any shortage of options. Indeed, there are more fly fishing possibilities on the West End during early autumn than any time of year.

Cutthroat are in virtually every river with access to tidewater. Chinook and early returning coho have returned to the Quillayute and rain forest rivers. The glacial rivers also host anadromous Dolly Varden/bull trout in autumn, fish so bright you can see through their fin rays. And the resident rainbow and cutthroat of Elk and Beaver, Wentworth and Pleasant lakes cruise the shallows, picking off flying ants and late season mayflies.

But early fall has a special meaning for Olympic Peninsula fly fishermen, because this is the season of summer steelhead and the floating line. In recent years, of course, more and more fishermen have begun to use floating lines year-round, even during winter. But the low flows and sun-warmed waters of Indian summer are perfect for the riffling hitch, waking and skating and the greased line. During September and October, fresh fish nose up into the Quillayute and rain forest rivers, joining the wild and hatchery fish that drifted in during the summer.

So I planned to keep fishing for steelhead. But as I neared the Smokehouse Restaurant, I still had a decision to make: Did I head for the upriver slicks and riffles on the Sol Duc or Calawah? Or did I want to fish the heavier water downstream?

I turned left onto the Mora Road. A few minutes later, I swung off the pavement onto a logging road. The road wound through a huge clear-cut at first, past enormous slash piles and dust-covered fireweed. I bounced over gravel washes and through mud puddles that had somehow survived two months of dry weather. Then it entered a dark, cool stand of timber. I drove on for a short distance farther, into another cut, then parked.

I wriggled into my waders, grabbed my vest and 7-weight and headed for the Calawah. Each fall, a modest run of hatchery steelhead swims up the Quillayute to the Bogachiel, then into the Calawah. Ranging from four to around 10 pounds, these Skamania stock fish are raised at the Bogachiel Rearing Ponds. It isn't a big run, and the low-water rock gardens and skin and bones rapids of autumn keep most drift boats off the river. The fish are pretty much left to locals and fly fishermen.

My forearms were scratched from

berry canes and I was sweating profusely from hiking in chest waders by the time I came to the river. After the midday heat of the clear-cut, the shade beneath the Sitka spruce and cedar was delightful. I sat on a moss-covered bed of sandstone and studied the river. The color of a wood sorrel petal held in the sun, it flowed glassily over grooved shelves for 30 feet, then widened into a gentle tailout. The ghostly shape of a steelhead hung above the sun-washed gravel at the head of the tailout.

I opened my fly box and found a low-water Lady Caroline. Perhaps more than any other Olympic Peninsula river, the Calawah presents anglers with the smooth flows and manageable currents that lend themselves to fishing the greased line. This is especially true in early autumn. And like every other Northwestern fly fisherman who has read and reread Roderick Haig-Brown, I cannot look at a summer steelhead in thin water without thinking of swinging a sparsely dressed wet fly in the surface film.

As for my fly selection, Haig-Brown, as always, said it best: "For greased-line fishing," he wrote in *The Western Angler*, "I think only two flies are necessary, the Blue Charm and the Lady Caroline; even the Blue Charm is probably superfluous..."

So I dressed my double taper, added a couple of feet to the leader from the Hoh and tied on the fly. Wading carefully and keeping a low profile, I moved into position above the ledge. I false cast several times to work out the correct amount of line, then cast across and slightly downstream. I tossed a couple of mends to slow the down-stream drift of the line. It was nerve-wracking, watching the fly move ever so slowly toward the slot, and I was strongly tempted to glance toward the fish. But I kept my eyes on the fly, following it with my rod tip.

As it neared the end of the swing, the fly began to move laterally toward the fish. Now I could see both the fly and the gray shadow. The steelhead hit just as the fly began to drag, to twitch across the current seam. It hit the fly hard and going away, and I didn't have to even think about setting the hook. It raced downstream, peeling off 60 feet of line, then somersaulted twice.

Ten minutes later, I slid the fish up onto the beach. It was five or six pounds, a pretty hen with the faint green on its back and splash of red on its gill plates that indicated it had been in the river for a while. Its adipose fin was snubbed and hard, though. I picked up a thick piece of driftwood. After silently memorizing the way the fish looked and thanking it, I killed it.

I was tired. Part of me wanted to carry the fish back to the truck and head for home. But there were two good stretches of fly water downstream. And I knew that the fall rains could begin any day. They would end greased-line fishing for another year. So I filled in my punch card, picked up the steelhead and waded back into the river.

As I picked my way downstream, I thought of another line Haig-Brown had written on fishing the greased-line. "It is enough to say that summer steelhead will respond to the method," he wrote, "and that the streams of the country lend themselves to it almost perfectly."

Chapter 13

October
Caddis

It was late September, before the first heavy autumn rains, and the Humptulips River looked like club soda flowing through a glass of crushed ice. But the slanting, late-afternoon light created a patchwork of light and shadow over the water. From my hiding place behind an alder snag, I could see a crimson vine maple leaf spinning lazily above the bottom of a sun-washed pool. But 30 feet downstream, the shady, slow water beneath the crown of the snag was dark and impenetrable.

Under most circumstances, you add several feet to your leader and drop down a couple of sizes on the fly when the water is low and clear. It's also the time to fish the fly as naturally as possible, to keep drag and movement to an absolute minimum. If you're smart, you won't arrive at the river until the sun is off the water. And even then you will crawl up to the edge of the river on your hands and knees and cast from behind trees and rocks.

But not always. My leader was only about seven feet long on the Humptulips that afternoon, tapered down to a fairly robust 4X tippet. Moreover, shadows wouldn't cover the river completely for several hours. I had run hunched-over to my cover behind the snag. But my fly was nearly two inches long—just about the size of the October caddis hovering above the river.

I stripped two loose coils of my double-taper, backcast, then shot the line downstream. It wasn't an especially artful presentation, the leader landing in sort of a pile in the middle of the tailout below the pool. But the current straightened it out quickly and carried it across-stream, toward the top of the snag. I tossed a mend, and the fly drifted into the slow, shady water on a slack line. I twitched the fly twice.

A fish slashed at the Orange Stimulator. I struck back with the rod. Feeling the hook, the fish thrashed on the surface. It had the dark back and amber sides of a cutthroat, a large one. I couldn't move down the bank because of the alder, so I waded out into the river. The fish bore back into the cover of fallen alder.

Within seconds, it was tangled. Then, remembering something I had read years before, I fed a coil of line downstream. Sure enough, several moments later the fish swam free. I kept it away from the tree from then on and gradually worked it upstream. It was at least two pounds, a pepper-spotted beauty, with a trace of its crimson throat slash coming back. I released it.

In Gary LaFontaine's classic, *Caddisflies*, he writes: "The question for fly fishermen seeking big trout is: 'Which insects provide the best opportunity for catching such fish?' My list would be: Giant Orange Sedge (*Dicosmoecus* sp.), Salmon Fly (*Pteronarcys californica*, a stonefly), and the Michigan Mayfly (*Hexagenia limbata*). *Dicosmoecus* is the most important—and the contest is not even close."

Now, that is a fairly unequivocal statement—one I agree with, having fished the Au Sable on summer nights, the Yellowstone in July and Olympic Peninsula rivers in autumn. But October caddis take on an added significance on peninsula rivers because they present just about the only opportunity to "match the hatch" for steelhead and sea-run cutthroat. Indeed, the emergence of the Olympic's other large subaquatic insects—the salmonflies and golden stones—tends to be ignored by adult steelhead and takes place before cutthroat are usually in the river. But the low water and fluttering egg-laying flights of the October caddis often draw the gaze of even the most wizened migratory trout to the surface.

If you have never seen an adult October caddis, they are impossible to mistake for anything else. Holding their wings over their bodies in a tent-shape and with the long antennae of all caddis, *Dicosmoecus* are much larger than any other Northwestern Trichoptera, approximately one and a half inches in length. Their bodies are orangish, their wings brown with dark venation. They are most common on relatively fast, boulder-strewn sections of larger rivers.

I have observed October caddis on a number of Olympic Peninsula rivers besides the Humptulips. In my opinion, the best hatches occur on the Quillayute rivers and the Elwha. ". . . I found both adult insects and steelhead," LaFontaine writes of a day he spent on the Sol Duc. "I stayed a day and fished this stream, the combination of dry flies and sea-run rainbows offering a fly-fishing opportunity too good to pass by. I did not hook any of the larger fish, the ten- to twelve-pounders that were rolling, but with a Bucktail Caddis I caught some smaller steelhead, and these fish were definitely feeding on the natural Giant Orange Sedge." Sol Duc, Calawah and Bogachiel cutthroat hit these large Trichoptera even more reliably than steelhead, often ambushing them from the slack water beneath overhanging alders.

Migratory fish still can't get around the dams on the Elwha. But ovipositing October caddis often produce extraordinary fishing for the resident rainbow of the Elwha backcountry. This is also the most pleasant time of year to hike into the upper river. The trails are much less crowded, for one thing. And although the nights are both longer and cooler in autumn, nearly all of the Elwha River backcountry is at low enough elevation that fires are permitted. Watching the orange fingers of fire play over a driftwood fire is a wonderful way to cap off a day of wilderness fly fishing.

Perhaps because their beds are so regularly scoured by floods, the *Dicosmoecus* hatches on the rain forest rivers seem sparser and more unpredictable than on other peninsula rivers. Nonetheless, I know several places on the Hoh and Queets where I can usually find October caddis during dry weather. In my experience, large, nearly unsinkable patterns fished with action produce best on the glacial rivers. The last steelhead I took on the Queets, for instance, fell to a Bomber worked across a fan of slick water on a riffled hitch.

There are a number of readily available patterns that serve admirably as *Dicosmoecus* imitations. When I first began fishing the hatch a number of years ago, I used a low-water Muddler Minnow. Originally created by Don Gapen to imitate the cottus minnows of the Lake Superior watershed, a Muddler isn't particularly representative of the fall caddis. Yet it was responsible for my first "dry fly" steelhead, a 10-pound Sol Duc native.

In succeeding years, I have tried a number of patterns designed specifically to imitate the insects, including Bill Bakke's October Caddis and Bill McMillan's Fall Caddis. I have also fished Bombers, Lani Waller's Waller Waker, large orange-bodied Humpies and Stimulators during autumn. They are all excellent flies, and I have had success with all of them at one time or another. To tell you the truth, I fish whatever I have in my vest when October caddis hover above the river.

*More than 40 rivers radiate out to tidewater from the
Olympic Peninsula's mountainous core.*

Ron Link skates a dry fly on a glacial river in autumn.

Anglers that hit the rain forest rivers between the rains of winter and early summer run-off often find them surprisingly low and clear.

The Hoh, Queets and Quinault valleys host the Northern Hemisphere's only true temperate zone rain forests.

A Sol Duc River summer coho negotiates the Salmon Cascades in Olympic National Park. (photo courtesy of the National Park Service)

Sawtooth ridges tower above the author on a remote lake in the Mount Skokomish Wilderness Area.

Running water is the vehicle and medium of all life on the Olympic Peninsula.

The author casts for sea-run cutthroat on a Strait of Juan de Fuca estuary.

This Eastern brook trout was taken from a montane zone lake a short time after ice out.

All five species of North American Pacific salmon, winter and summer steelhead, sea-run cutthroat, Dolly Varden, and bull trout return to Olympic Peninsula rivers.

Although most precipitation on West End rivers falls as rain, snow blankets rain forest and Quillayute River valleys several times each winter.

The author works a nymph on a favorite northern Hood Canal beaver pond.

October caddis time on the Hoh River near the Olympic National Park boundary.

Ron Link prepares to release a native rain forest winter steelhead.

Before the construction of the Elwha Dam in 1912, the Elwha River was one of the most productive anadromous fish systems on the West Coast. Today its sockeye, spring Chinook and pink salmon are extinct, and its surviving stocks are all classified as "critical."

*The healthiest stocks of Chinook salmon and winter steelhead in the lower 48 states
return to protected headwater spawning grounds in Olympic National Park.*

The petroglyphs near Cape Alava are mute testimony to the significance fish and shell-fish played in the lives of ancient Olympic coastal societies.

Spent salmon carcasses are the foundation of a rich web of life in the Olympics, feeding more than 27 species of wildlife.

The author took this "dip in" hatchery summer steelhead from a rain forest river. Note he wears hiking boots rather than waders.

Sea-run cutthroat are available on the large West End rivers from early July through late fall; they often gather in slack water beneath overhanging vegetation.

Exposed gravel bars and low water mean that it is time for dry lines and summer steelhead.

Water falling over rock is the music of the Olympics.

Lake Ozette

T he Makah Indians called it Ka'houk, which means "large body of fresh water." "A vast, watery crater in the forest," is how novelist Ivan Doig described 8-1/2-mile-long, 7,787-acre Lake Ozette in *Winter Brothers*, his chronicle of nineteenth century Olympic Peninsula historian and ethnologist James Swan. According to tradition, Swan was the first European American to see the lake, traveling south along the coast with the Makahs in July of 1864 to Cape Alava, then hiking three miles inland to the lake. Although Swan had no way of knowing it, the lake he beheld that day is the largest lake on the Olympic Peninsula and the third largest natural lake in Washington. It also holds the distinction of being both the most western and most northwestern large lake in the conterminous United States.

Ironically, visitors conditioned to the calendar-art drama of Northwestern stillwaters like Oregon's Wallowa Lake and the Olympic Peninsula's Lake Crescent are often surprised, sometimes even disappointed, by Lake Ozette. Float-tube anglers familiar with lakes like Central Oregon's Little Lava or Lenice Lake in the Columbia Basin, similarly, often find Ozette incomprehensible. Indeed, marshy, tea-colored Ozette, dimpled by rain and churned by wind, framed by its spongy shoreline, thickly-timbered hills and coastal mist and fog, often presents a somber, even grave, aspect.

It is an aspect that also sometimes seems peculiarly non-Northwestern. "I keep expecting to see a moose," I remarked to a friend the first time I fished the lake. And this remote lake—it is more than 20 miles to the nearest store and the ranger station and rangers' dwellings are the only buildings along its shore—sometimes seems to have been plopped down from the Maine woods or the Canadian Shield.

A list of the fish that inhabit Ozette, however, reveals that it is a classic Northwestern body of water, even so far as harboring a few exotics. Sockeye salmon, which provided a rich fishery for the Makah Tribe until the late 1950s and which are currently the subject of an intensive restoration program, arrive in late summer and early fall. Coho and chum salmon swim up the Ozette River, the lake's outlet, during fall and early winter. Bound for spawning tributaries like Big River and Umbrella Creek, steelhead pass through the lake each winter. Sculpin, stickleback, peamouth and squawfish live in the lake year-round, as do nonnative largemouth bass and yellow perch.

But the most productive and dependable fly fishing on Lake Ozette is for the cutthroat trout that return to the lake each autumn. "The lake has a substantial population of cutthroat," explains Olympic National Park fisheries biologist John Meyer. According to Meyer, most of the cutthroat in the lake are anadromous, returning from the ocean during summer and early fall. These fish often remain in the lake for extended periods before finally committing to their spawning streams. In addition to sea-runs, Meyer says Lake Ozette also contains a small population of resident coastal cutthroat.

Most of the cutthroat I have taken from Ozette have fallen to a streamer towed behind a rowboat or a canoe. In case you aren't aware of it, trolling flies isn't considered "fly fishing" by the folks that certify record fish. But I have always believed Lee Wulff's observation that the difference between a sport and a game is you don't keep score in a sport. On a lake the size of

Ozette, trolling is just about the only practical way to approach the fish—at least, until you locate a school of trout.

But I also like to troll—in a canoe or rowboat without power, that is. I like its tradition, the fact that it evolved on the "squaretail" and land-locked salmon flowages of nineteenth century New England. I like the flies; patterns like the Gray Ghost and Black Nosed Dace are as beautiful as they are functional. The boats—the incredibly stable Rangely Lakes freighter canoes and the graceful cedar strip canoes—also appeal to my techno-phobic nature. Finally, I expect I will be able to wield oars and paddles long after my jogging-ruined knees can no longer negotiate glacial rivers or beaver ponds.

Much of what I know about trolling I picked up from a small 1977 book, *Trout Hunting*, by Frank Woolner. Best known as an editor of *Saltwater Sportsmen* magazine and for his writing on grouse and woodcock hunting, Woolner is also an avid and knowledgeable trout fisherman. Woolner is one of my favorite outdoor writers because, like Ted Trueblood and Charlie Watermens, he is more concerned with the setting, creatures and narrative of sport than the gear.

From Woolner, I learned that a level sinking line is better for trolling than a floating line because it keeps the fly just under the surface. I also learned to use a much longer leader than I would have thought, typically around 20 feet. And I discovered that a streamer pattern should match the forage species of a lake at least as well as a nymph or dry fly mimics insects on a stream.

However, I hadn't yet read *Trout Hunting* on the late September day I took my first Lake Ozette cutthroat. Looking back, I think I was simply "given" that fish, as sometimes seems to happen. Maybe this is the way the gods kindle an enthusiasm or blow sparks on a flagging one.

I had borrowed a friend's canoe and made the long drive from Port Townsend out to the lake. It was an exhilarating trip,

beneath crisp blue skies, with red and gold foliage decorating the banks of the Pysht and Hoko rivers. The aluminum hulls of cartoppers on the Strait of Juan de Fuca winked in the sun.

Unfortunately, the sun had disappeared beneath the tree tops by the time I pulled into the campground at the north end of the lake. I was eager to fish, but I made camp first. I set up the dome tent, spread out the sleeping bags and pad, and split the firewood I had brought from home. Then I wrestled the canoe off the top of the car.

I figured I had about 45 minutes of light left. It hardly seemed worth the effort to launch the canoe for such a short amount of time, especially since I had always heard that the most productive cutthroat fishing was many miles to the south. But I was in the mood to fish, so I dragged the canoe over to the launch and pushed off past the tules. I stretched my leader and tied on a Black Nosed Dace. I fed out line until most of my double taper trailed behind the canoe.

Paddling on alternate sides of the canoe, I was able to keep a fairly straight course. I planned to fish the small bays where Umbrella Creek and Big Creek empty into the lake the next day. With the color quickly fading from the sky, however, I pointed the bow in the direction of Deer Point, roughly a mile and a half distant. The upper body exercise felt good after three hours in the car, but I didn't see any signs of fish.

I made it to the point faster than I thought I would. The brilliant blue of the afternoon sky had faded to a pale clamshell color, but the clouds that often drift in from the ocean just before sunset hadn't materialized. I was tempted to try for the mouth of Umbrella Creek, which I guessed was less than a mile away. But it was fall, and the long twilights of summer were gone. As it was, I probably wouldn't get back to camp until after dark.

So I dug in on the port side and swung the canoe back toward the campground. As my fly line flared across the tip of the point,

I glanced back to make sure it didn't snag the shoreline. I saw the line stretch tightly, then a swirl beneath the fly.

I grabbed the rod, but the line was slack. Completely on impulse, I stripped twice. I felt the sharp tap of a striking fish and set the hook. The fish boiled on the surface for an instant, then slashed through the shallows, shaking its head, staying low. I knew it was a cutthroat.

It was a very vigorous fish, and after a while I began to fantasize about how big it would be. Seventeen inches, I wondered?. Maybe more? With most of my fly line out, it took me a while to bring the fish to the boat. When I did, I was surprised to see that it was only about 15 inches, if that. Even more surprising was its appearance. I think I had been half expecting Ozette Lake cutthroat to carry the somber, murky colors of the lake. But this was as bright as any cutthroat I had ever seen. Except for its sprinkling of black spots, it could have passed for a summer-bright sockeye.

I worked the barbless hook from the corner of its jaw. As the fish rested on the palm of my hand, I wondered when it had abandoned the kelp and reefs of the coast for the dark amber water of the Ozette River. Not long ago, I thought, for it to be this bright. Suddenly its gill plates pulsed twice, then its entire body shuddered. It swam free.

It was now that watery half light that precedes total darkness. I reeled in the loose fly line from the bottom of the canoe and stashed the rod against the bow seat. Taking up the paddle, I saw a coyote on the shore. It had a lush brindle coat and the sharp intelligent features of its species. Our eyes met, and we held each other's gaze for a long time. Then it disappeared into the thickets of salal that bind the shoreline.

A bat swooped over the bow of the canoe. Two yellow lights flickered at the rangers' quarters, more than a mile distant. They were comforting, but for some reason I shuddered. I dug the paddle into the dark water and pointed the bow toward the light.

Chapter 15

Hooked
Noses

It wasn't the first time I had heard this story. Indeed, I had been hearing about people taking jack salmon on dry flies for as long as I had lived on the peninsula.

"It was unbelievable," he said.

I didn't know his name, never would. He approached me as I updated the message board in the sporting goods store where I worked.

"There were about 12 fish in this deep pool," he continued. "I thought they were silvers, at first."

"Which river, did you say?"

"It was the Hoh. Up near the park boundary."

I put the cap on the felt pen. "And you got them on dry flies?" I asked, trying not to sound incredulous.

"Just the first one," he replied. "Like I was saying, they were in this deep pool. I figured I should use something like a Silver Hilton. I've taken silvers on them in the past. But I had heard about people taking them on dries. And these fish seemed really fresh and active."

"What did you use?" By now, I had come to the conclusion that this guy wasn't one of those characters that have to impress everyone with their largely imaginary fishing triumphs.

"Well, I thought about a Stimulator, because I already had one drying on my vest," he said. "But it seemed too big, too bushy for the pool. I ended up using a number 6 black Bomber."

He told me he crept into position at the head of the pool. Then he dropped the fly a few yards upstream of the salmon. Feeding line from the slack in his left hand, he floated it down to the fish.

"The lead fish smacked it," he said, excitedly. "Even though I could see the whole thing, I could hardly believe it."

But he was even more surprised when he brought the fish to hand and discovered that it was not a coho, but a jack Chinook.

"After that first fish, the whole school was fidgety and they wouldn't hit the dry fly. I rested them for a while, then switched to a small Fall Favorite. I got the other two on that."

Well, that was enough to prime my pump. Unfortunately, the very next day a storm knocked the lingering Olympic Peninsula Indian summer into history. For nearly a week, clouds the color of a three-day-old black eye scudded across the lowlands. Trailing cold rain and wild gusts of wind, the storm stripped the last leaves from the trees and knocked out power lines.

Five days after the rain stopped, the rain forest rivers and Quillayute system were still churning soups of leaves, mud and opaque gray water. The Elwha and the Dosewallips were also out, as was the Humptulips, one of the peninsula's finest salmon streams.

When I called down to Montesano, however, I learned that the rivers of the southern Olympics—the Satsop, Wynoocheee, and Wishkah—were high but fishable.

"With flies?" I pressed.

"Maybe. If you hurry."

"What do you mean?" I asked.

"I just heard that another big storm is blowing in."

I was on the road the next morning an hour before first light. Rain spattered my windshield and the boughs of the fir trees swayed wildly as I followed U.S. 101 down the west shore of Hood Canal. Passing the Hamma Hamma River, it occurred to me that it was probably snowing in the headwaters and that two of my favorite subalpine lakes would now be locked away for the winter. I pulled off at the Skokomish Indian Reservation for a cup of coffee.

After the long stretches of empty road along the canal, the brief flurry of traffic near Shelton seemed strange. It began to rain harder now, driven by wild gusts of wind from the southwest, the direction I was heading. I turned off onto the Shelton-Matlock Cutoff. A few minutes later I topped the ridge that is the divide between the Puget Sound basin and the Chehalis River watershed, which flows via Grays Harbor to the Pacific Ocean.

The only side of the Olympic Peninsula not bound by tidewater, the south flank of the Olympics is drained by the northern tributaries to the Chehalis—the Wishkah, Wynoochee and Satsop. When white settlers first pushed into the Chehalis Valley in the mid-nineteenth century, these murky, slow-moving rivers virtually throbbed with sea-run cutthroat, fall salmon and winter steelhead. A century of poor logging practices, overfishing and pollution of the estuary, however, resulted in an alarming decline in Chehalis fish runs by the end of the 1970s. But in what has become the peninsula's outstanding example of a cooperative fisheries restoration effort, private citizens, industry, the tribes and the state worked together to restore habitat and enhance the runs. Today, after decades of decline, many Chehalis watershed anadromous fish stocks have rebounded dramatically.

Unfortunately, there was less than a foot of visibility by the time I waded into the Satsop. My plan had been to slowly work my way downstream, hitting all of the promising fly water. But with horizontal sheets of rain blowing up the valley and the river rising quickly, I knew I would be lucky to get in an hour's fishing. I cut the leader on my sink tip back to three feet and tied on a heavy, fluorescent egg pattern. It struck me that this was about as far from fishing dry flies for jack Chinook as you could get and still be fly fishing for salmon.

On my very first cast, the wind caught the tapered part of my line on my backcast and blew it into my face—something that hadn't happened in 25 years of fly fishing. Then I heard a sharp, splintering sound. Looking upstream, I saw the top of a large fir slowly falling toward the river. Its boughs feathered the air, like the wings of a mallard braking into a slough, and it seemed to take a long time to fall. When the crown of the tree finally landed, it threw up a veil of gray water more than 20 feet high. The top of the tree trunk was jagged and pink.

I reeled in my fly line. A fisherman with a drift rod could possibly have cut through the wind with spoons or big spinners for an hour or so, until the river was completely out. But casting a fly line was out of the question. Besides, it seemed to be getting a little dangerous. I scrambled up the bank to the road, then hiked back to my truck.

Now, that's not a very instructive tale. But it does contain most of the elements I associate with fly fishing for salmon on Olympic Peninsula rivers—namely, other people's success stories, personal failure, treacherous weather and deteriorating river conditions. Don't get me wrong; fly fishermen take salmon on Olympic rivers. Jim Garrett created an effective series of patterns for coho, pinks and chum when he lived along the Dungeness River. And I have taken salmon from rain forest, Quillayute and Hood Canal rivers. But dour—the term anglers in the United Kingdom use to describe uncooperative Atlantic salmon—is a fairly optimistic way to describe most Olympic Peninsula salmon most of the time.

Moreover, the mid-October through early December return of coho salmon, the species most inclined to hit a fly in fresh water, happens to coincide with some of the worst weather of the year. Along the Satsop, more than 30 inches of rain can fall between the beginning of September and the end of November, 10 times as much as during the summer. It is even wetter on coastal rivers. During November of 1990, nearly 19 inches of rain fell within a 36-hour period at the Hoh Ranger Station. That is more than it normally rains in Port Townsend in an entire year. Obviously, the odds of taking a salmon on a fly diminish considerably when you can't see your wading shoes in a foot of water.

Still, I nearly always spend a few days each autumn on a river with an 8-weight in my hands. When it's not raining, it's a glorious time to be on a river, with the scarlet of the vine maple and butter-colored cottonwood leaves lighting up the river banks. And even when I don't connect with a salmon, I usually see them—humpbacked pinks and calico-flanked chum, bright coho and burly Chinook. Wading among these fish is a rite of an Olympic Peninsula autumn, one that connects me with one of the Pacific Northwest's most compelling and beautiful mysteries.

"In a region that has been reworked by waves of glaciers for the last million years and which otherwise counts leaching rains as its predominant meteorological phenomenon, the wild salmon serve as nature's principal means of returning nutrients from the sea to the land," Bruce Brown wrote in *Mountain in the Clouds*. "Through their passionate, seemingly perverse death, they give life not only to their own progeny but also to a host of predators and other dependent pieces. They are, in short, an engine of general enrichment, and an important element in the long range stability of the Pacific Coast ecosystem."

Chapter 16

Hatchery
Steelhead

It was the first week of December. I owed a magazine an article on early winter fishing on the Olympic Peninsula. Naturally enough, most of the piece focused on blackmouth salmon fishing on the eastern Strait of Juan de Fuca and steelhead fishing on the West End. I mentioned the Humps, Winter Hole and Midchannel Bank for the salmon fishermen, then ticked off the names of the rivers that host strong runs of early returning hatchery steelhead—the Lyre, the Salmon and the Bogachiel. I listed the last few years' harvest records for the rivers and the numbers of smolts planted two years earlier.

Wanting to tie the piece up with a quote, I called out to the Department of Fish and Wildlife's Bogachiel Rearing Pond in Forks and asked if any fish had shown up yet. "They sure have," exclaimed the hatchery manager. "I'll tell you, I have seen fish this early before. But I have never seen this many fish this early."

Now, before you panic and think I am going to begin waxing rhapsodically about hatchery steelhead, let me say that I regret that any were ever dumped into Olympic Peninsula rivers. In a paper he presented at the 1983 Olympic Wild Fish Conference, Washington Department of Natural Resources fish biologist Jeff Cederholm chronicled how native Sol Duc winter steelhead declined after the introduction of large numbers of Chambers Creek hatchery fish and an attendant increase in angling pressure. Once the local Trout Unlimited chapter convinced the state to discontinue plants on the Sol Duc and gave it permission to develop an enhancement program based entirely on hook-and-line-caught wild fish, the native stocks in the Sol Duc rebounded—despite continued heavy angling pressure. More than one-third of these native

Sol Duc winter steelhead are three-salt fish, in the 12- to 25-pound range, while less than five percent of the four- to seven-pound Chambers Creek steelhead spend three years at sea.

More recently, Kauffman's Streamborn employee Brian McLachlan submitted a report to the Washington Wildlife Commission demonstrating how heavy sport and tribal angling pressure directed at hatchery steelhead on the Quillayute System has resulted in an incidental yet severe overharvest of early-timed native steelhead. According to McLachlan's research, returns of natives to Quillayute tributaries in December and January have fallen from 35 percent or more of the total run to around 20 percent since the introduction of hatchery fish.

In my opinion, hatchery fish have also been largely responsible for several generations of anglers, politicians and academics that believe anadromous fish runs can be controlled mechanically, like feed lot cattle. This technology-based approach to fisheries management has, in turn, created an atmosphere where habitat destruction and overfishing can seem inconsequential. It also paved the way for the disastrous "in lieu of" arrangements on many rivers, where threatened stocks of steelhead and salmon were "replaced" by cultured non-native fish. The ultimate flowering of this arrogant and heedless approach to the stewardship of anadromous fish, of course, can be seen on the Columbia River, where one of the most bountiful salmonid systems on the planet has declined to the point that panicky managers and politicians now quible over which stocks are most endangered.

Perhaps more subtly, I think a good case can be made that hatchery runs of steelhead, along with refinements in bait-casting and spinning gear and the introduction of monofilament line, have in large part been responsible for the dramatic increase in the number of anglers pursuing the fish over the last few decades. When I talk to anglers that fished the Olympics 40 or 50 years ago, for example, they claim that the fishing was good, often extraordinary. But they also report that the steelhead drifted into the rivers throughout the season and spread through the entire system. Hatchery fish, on the other hand, return from saltwater within a very narrow window of time and typically exploit a small percentage of a watershed. This, obviously, makes them much easier to catch.

"Hatchery fish are for the wanna-bes," Olympic Sporting Goods' Bob Gooding says with characteristic bluntness. "Wild fish separate the men from the boys."

Having said all this, I must admit that I am never disappointed when I beach a steelhead and notice that its adipose or ventral fin is short and stubby. As I've said before, I like to eat fish. And there are few fish that taste as a good as steelhead. I like it steaked and barbecued. I like it filleted and sautéed in garlic and butter. I like to bake an entire fish Spanish-style, in a bed of tomatoes, olives, onions, mushrooms and garlic. And since hatchery fish are the only steelhead I kill—my biologist friends actually encourage the practice—I am happy when I catch one.

A lot of them return to Olympic Peninsula rivers in December and January. In 1993, more than 1,750,000 winter steelhead smolts were planted in 26 Olympic rivers. At a modest two percent return rate that, theoretically, results in more than 35,000 fish returning to the peninsula. Along the coast, they return to Indian rivers like the Sail and Sooes, to large rivers like the Quillayute and to small rivers like Goodman Creek. Two- and three-salt fish also nose up into the Chehalis' northern tributaries—the Hoquiam, Wishkah, Wynoochee and Satsop—and to Grays Harbor's Humptulips. Despite more than a decade of wretched returns, the state still

dumps them into the Hood Canal rivers. The Elwha S'Klallam, the Makah and the Washington Department of Fish and Wildlife plant eight rivers that drain into the Strait of Juan de Fuca.

But no river on the Olympic Peninsula is more identified with hatchery steelhead than the Bogachiel. Indeed, despite its location on the West End of the peninsula, more than five hours from Seattle, the Bogachiel is one of the three or four most productive winter steelhead rivers in the state. During typical winters it yields between 2,500 and 4,000 fish to sportsmen between Thanksgiving and the end of January, most of them originating from the Bogachiel Rearing Ponds, located just above the confluence of the Bogey and the Calawah. The Quileute tribe also harvests between 3,000 and 5,000 of the highly cultured Bogachiel fish. Any way you look at it, this is a lot of steelhead.

It is also not a secret. From Thanksgiving weekend to the end of January, the lower Bogachiel is beaten to a froth by sport fishermen. The lower river was too crowded for me 10 years ago when most of the fishermen were local. In recent years, as Puget Sound steelhead runs have foundered, Seattle outdoor writers have given the Bogachiel enough ink to float a ferry boat. And during Fridays in December and January, scores of urban anglers ride the Klickitat and Chelan across the predominately "steelhead-free zone" of Central Puget Sound. This is understandable, and I would do the same thing if my home water was an I-5 river. But it's a different type of fishery along the Bogachiel these days, an ugly Clockwork Orange sort of steelheading, with trash and cigarette smoke, temper tantrums and beer cans.

So I don't usually fish the Bogachiel early in the season. Hell, I never fish the Bogachiel early in the season. But after I hung up the phone with the biologist, I began to play around with the notion of making a quick trip to the West End. You see, the Hoh, one drainage south of the

Bogachiel, also hosts a hatchery run of winter steelhead. Moreover, the vast, wide-open spaces of the section of the Hoh below the Highway 101 bridge are much better suited to fly fishing than the trees and high banks of the lower Bogachiel. Also, most anglers avoid the Hoh in early winter, accepting the conventional wisdom that it is pretty much a March and early April show.

The trick to fishing the Hoh in early winter is to hit it when it is in shape. "Fast moving white water" is the translation of the Indian name Hoh, and that is usually an apt description of the river in early winter. More than 40 inches of rain typically falls on the rain forest between the first of November and the end of January. This is the time of year when the Hoh and the other rain forest rivers recreate themselves (the lower Queets and Quinault are on the Quinault Indian Reservation and tribal guides must be employed). It's when the rivers cut new tailouts and fill in old pools. It's when the huge snags that end up among the jackstraw piles of logs along the coast are carried to sea. Standing by the Hoh after two or three days of rain is like standing by a train track as a coal train pulls up an Appalachian valley.

Sooner or later, however, the rain stops. Sometimes there are only a few days between fronts. When that happens, only the tribal fishermen and the plunkers venture forth. But there are longer dry spells in December and January as well, when the river drops into plug and drift-fishing condition. And usually at least one time during early winter, a stretch of dry weather will coincide with a sharp cold snap. When that happens—when the river is within its banks and there is a foot or so of visibility and the glaciers are locked-up—it's time to slap the chains on your vehicle and head west. Believe me, it won't last.

The day I talked to the Bogachiel manager happened to occur at the end of a week of cold, dry weather. A warming trend and snow were predicted, however, so I decided to hit the Hoh while the conditions were still good. The stars were twinkling brightly when I went to bed, and I remember thinking, "No snow tomorrow." But I sensed something different when I woke up the next morning—a stillness, a rapt sort of silence. Raising the blinds, I saw a luminous skiff of snow covering the yard. I got dressed quickly in the dark and made a sandwich.

Fortunately, the snow was wet, and Eaglemount, Gardiner and Fairholm hills, stretches that are normally worrisome in the snowy darkness, were in good shape. By the time I reached Bear Creek, a few miles east of Beaver, there were as many vehicles towing drift boats as passenger vehicles and log trucks combined. But the red tail lights on all of the boat trailers turned onto the roads that lead down to ramps on the Bogachiel. I continued south, topping the ridge between the Bogachiel and Hoh just as the first streaky orange and gold filaments of light broke over the jagged peaks of Mount Olympus.

A half-hour later, I parked my car at the turnaround at the end of the Oil City Road, a mile or so from the river mouth. There were no other vehicles in the parking area and no guide boats within sight. We have some of the best fly fishing guides in the state on the Olympic Peninsula, knowledgeable and eloquent wild fish advocates like Bob Pigott, J.D. Love and Herb Jacobsen. But there is no love lost between most sport anglers and the growing horde of plug pullers and bait bouncers that set up shop on West End rivers each winter. A good friend of mine began pitching his spoon at the head of a guide's client after the guide tried to muscle him out of a pool. A different friend had a gun pulled on him when he objected to the guide's anchoring his boat in the middle of the water he was fishing.

My approach to guides is less extravagant. Basically, I fish the lower sections of rivers at first light, before the drift-boat anglers and guides have a chance to launch and float down to them. That way, I usually have at least an hour or so of peace and quiet—or at least only wading fishermen to deal with. Then I move upstream, above the hatchery outlets and boat ramps. The farther you go upstream—and many Olympic Peninsula rivers are open to winter steelheading well beyond the end of the roads—the fewer people you encounter. And although you would think that few fish would survive the early winter gauntlet of nets, guide boats and sport anglers in the lower rivers, I enjoy much of my most memorable fishing upriver.

There was no snow on the lower Hoh that morning, probably a reflection of its proximity to the ocean. Walking across the immense gray expanse of Barlow's Bar, I passed windrows of bleached snags. On the other side of the river, a picket line of lichen-covered alders stood before a taller, darker backdrop of Sitka spruce and cedar. Drifts of low gray clouds, as sodden as dishrags, rolled in from the coast. It wasn't exactly raining, but as is so often the case along the coast, a heavy mist or drizzle, whatever you want to call it, oozed from the atmosphere. When I stood still and listened carefully, I could hear the muffled cadence of the surf.

I waded into the head of a run where I have taken not only steelhead, but coho, cutthroat and Dolly Varden/bull trout in the past. Tugging at my wading shoes and pushing hard on the back of my calves, the Hoh was, nonetheless, low and clear for a glacial river in winter. I snapped a sink tip spool into my reel, then tied on a leech pattern. After a couple of swings, I realized the fly wasn't getting anywhere near the bottom. I stripped the line in, removed the leader and looped a one-foot section of lead core to the end of the sink tip. I reattached the same leader but replaced the leech with a Bead Chain Comet.

Like many things that are now important in my life—playing Bach, running, gardening—the downstream wet-fly swing held little appeal for me initially. My early experience as a fly fisherman was primarily as a hatch-matcher and nymph fisherman, and I thought the downstream swing was boring and simple-minded. But I eventually

came to realize that virtually every combination of water, weather and season demands different line choices, fly choices and angles of presentation. Once I understood this, I began to take more fish than when I used the same line and fly all day. In time, I even began to appreciate the rather pleasant combination of contemplation, deliberation and rhythm that is the wet-fly swing.

On this winter morning, however, there wasn't much time for contemplation. Indeed, a fish smashed the fly on my first pass with the new terminal gear. I swung back on the rod and a quicksilver-bright five- or six-pounder exploded from the gray water. It jumped three times, writhing, head-over-heels leaps, then it streaked downstream. Splashing into the shallows, I followed it down to the end of the run where the river broke over a shallow riffle.

I regained a few feet of line as the steelhead paused momentarily. Then it raced back upstream. I cranked madly on my reel handle, trying to keep slack off the water. The fish jumped again, then tailwalked across the current. When I pumped tentatively on the rod, it shook its head and headed back downstream.

By now, I had begun to wonder if I had a hatchery fish or a native. And as the fight dragged on—down into the rocky shallows of the riffle, up into the deep green water behind a cedar sweeper—I became more and more certain that I had hooked one of those small, early-returning firecracker natives. I brought it up into the shallows three times before I finally was able to tail it and slide it up onto the gray sand. Its fins were flawless.

When I stood up after releasing the fish, I saw that a guide had taken up position at the head of the run. Although the guide and his two clients were only about 20 yards away, we didn't acknowledge each other's presence. I also noticed two fishermen moving across the bar toward the river. I reeled in my line, broke down my rod and began the long walk back to my truck.

Chapter 17

Cedar
Creeks

W hen I look back through my fishing journals, I am often struck by
how patterns of activity emerge,
patterns that I was largely unaware of when
I was engaged in them. This always surpris-
es me, because it is an article of faith with
me that there is a cyclical inevitability to my
angling year. If it's winter it's steelhead, in
other words; if it's summer it's trout. But
when you think about it, categories like
"steelhead" and "trout" are too broad to
have any real meaning on a place with the
diversity of the Olympic Peninsula. After all,
I can fish for trout in estuaries, glacial rivers
and alpine lakes, with floating lines or sink
tips, Wooly Buggers or chironomid pupae.
And although winter fishing opportunities
are more restricted, I still have enormous
latitude in where, how and when I want to
fish. So I guess it stands to reason the places
I lived, the friends I had and the books I
read shaped the way I fished during different periods of my life.

Interestingly, I can almost always dis-
cern the catalyst behind the patterns in my
journals. For example, I spent an awful lot of
time fishing soft hackle flies and caddis patterns on the upper Elwha and Graywolf
after reading Sylvester Neymes and Gary
LaFontaine's books. On the other hand,
when I lived on Hood Canal I tended to concentrate on beaver ponds and sea-runs during the summer. And when I pull the oldest,
most faded pages from my writing desk, I
always rediscover that I spent many of my
early days on the Olympic Peninsula fishing
the small, cedar-stained creeks that feed into
the western strait and the coast.

Rising on peaks and ridges too low to
support permanent snowfields, let alone
glaciers, these short-run rivers are fed by
springs, rainfall and intermittent brief snow.
Some are associated with geographically dis-

tinct features, Muller Mountain for the Twin
rivers, Stolzenberg Mountain for the Pysht.
But most of these streams—the Clallam and
Seiku, Goodman and Mosquito creeks, the
Dickey and the Hoko—drain nameless
1,500- to 3,000-foot coastal foothills. Far
from the mountainous core of the Olympics,
they wind through dense "dog hair" fir, dim
alder bottoms and the cedar swamps that
give them their characteristic iced-tea color.
With the exception of the Hoko, whose
upper reaches are now set aside as fly-only
water for winter steelhead, few
Northwestern anglers have heard much
about these slow, brush-bound rivers. Sea-
run cutthroat are the principle attraction for
the fly fisherman, but they also host various
combinations of Chinook, coho and chum
salmon, as well as modest runs of native and
hatchery winter steelhead.

In retrospect, I understand why I spent
so many hours on the Pysht and Hoko during my first years on the peninsula: The
scope of the cedar creeks was similar to the
Rocky Mountain streams I was familiar
with, even if the water color wasn't. Unlike
the large West End rivers, which took me
much longer to decipher with a fly rod, I
could see where the fish would lie on the
cedar creeks and I knew how to approach
them. I fished for the sea-run cutthroat of
late summer and fall and the coho of
October. And after a few obligatory trips to
the Sol Duc or Calawah each winter, I usually retreated back to the water I understood.

I don't have to look at my notes to
remember the first winter steelhead I
hooked on a fly. It was the third week of
December, a day or two before the winter
solstice. Most steelhead fishermen were on
the Bogachiel, the Lyre or the Elwha, trying
to derrick a hatchery fish up onto the bank.

In an attempt to avoid the crowds—and to find room for a backcast—I had swung off Highway 101 a few miles west of Port Angeles onto State Route 112. One of the peninsula's most scenic routes, 112 winds along the north shore of the peninsula for 40 miles to its terminus near Cape Flattery, the northwestern tip of the lower 48 states. Meandering west, the road climbs spurs that offer breathtaking views of the Strait of Juan de Fuca and Vancouver Island. It also drops down to cross more than half a dozen cedar creeks.

I began the day on the lower Hoko, the section along the Ozette-Hoko Road downstream from the fly area. I remember that I was struck by how much the river and the scenery had changed since my last trip for sea-runs in early November. In late autumn, coho, chum and a few kings still thrashed through the tailouts and rolled in the pocket pools. A handful of golden cottonwood and brassy-colored maple leaves clung to the streamside trees. And although the sky was low and gray, heavy with the promise of months of rain, it was still a summer river then, with a pulse that was hard to detect.

The buffetting of late fall storms had transformed the Hoko. It hurried past the gravel bars and alder bottoms now, carrying liverish salmon carcasses downstream. Only a few fungus-covered chum were still alive. The streamside cottonwoods were bare, while the yellow-green club moss that adorned the maples seemed more prominent. You could see your breath in the shady spots, and the frost clung to the sword fern throughout the day.

I parked at a turnout above the river. I worked my way downstream, carefully fishing four or five spots I had found while cutthroat fishing. After more than two hours, the only action I had was a terminal chum that chomped onto the fly, then floated downstream like a piece of driftwood. Shortly before noon, I crunched through an alder bottom and hiked back to my truck.

I drove to the Sekiu River, the next river to the west. I have always been intrigued by the Sekiu, probably because I know next to nothing about it. I spent an hour driving around looking for fly water and access without success. Then I ate my peanut butter, cheese and onion sandwich—a variation on the "elk hunt specials" described in Craig Leslie's novel *Winterkill.* I watched an otter patrol the pool above the 112 bridge.

By now, it was mid-afternoon. The flat winter light had already begun to fade. I drove back to Clallam Bay and bought a bottle of pop. I had planned to fish both the Clallam and Pysht rivers on my way home, but didn't have enough daylight left for both rivers. I passed over the Clallam and drove to the section of the Pysht on the Merrill-Ring Tree Farm. This was before Merrill-Ring charged for access to their land. I parked in a turnout beneath an immense, blue-green Sitka spruce.

I followed a muddy, overgrown two-track downstream. I kicked up a thick-necked blacktail buck and watched it bound away, its quirky, stiff-legged gait carrying it into the forest. The Pysht, like the Hoko and Sekiu, was high but clear. I scrambled down to a gravel bar on the shallow side of a small pool. Keeping a low profile, I positioned myself directly across from a deep cutbank on the opposite side of the river.

I checked my knot and discovered that the hook on my Purple Peril was dull. For no particular reason, I tied on a Polar Shrimp. I cast a few yards above the cutbank. The sink tip carried the fly and short leader down quickly. I tossed a tight upstream mend just before the line drifted into the deep water. After it bounced through the slot, I let it drift downstream, then carefully stripped it back in.

The fish hit on the next pass. Up until then, all of my steelhead had come on drift gear, where the take can be very slight. But this was a real strike, as definite as a ringing telephone. I struck back. A black-backed, silver-sided fish wallowed across the surface of the pool. I struck again, just to make sure. The fish raced downstream, peeling line from my small reel. I splashed downstream behind it.

It would be nice to say I landed that first fly-rod steelhead. It would be nice, but it wouldn't be true. No, the fish took out about 40 feet of line on its first run. That carried it into the next pool downstream. In the excitement, I forgot everything I had read about playing steelhead. I tried to play it like a trout, stripping in the slack line that I regained by chasing it. Unfortunately, there was still about a half-dozen feet of line lying on the water when it jumped. The hook beat the fish back to the water by about two seconds.

Oddly enough, I wasn't particularly upset. Actually, the experience gave me a new, heightened enthusiasm for winter steelhead fly fishing. It's a good thing, too, because another year would pass before I took my first winter fish on a fly. It was a six-pounder, as bright as a burnished chalice. It hit a fluorescent egg pattern. It was a Cedar Creek fish.

Although it nourishes delicate flowers, ferns and moss, the running water of the Olympic Peninsula is also its sculptor, carving out valleys and stream beds from solid rock.

Chapter 18

Winter
Cutthroat

An hour earlier, Ron Link and I had eaten lunch at the Corner House Restaurant in Port Angeles, within walking distance of the ferry to Victoria and beneath the frozen leer of a mounted 60-pound king salmon. Now, we picked our way across a sodden patch of pickleweed and tidal mud, following a creek down to the flat water of its estuary on the Strait of Juan de Fuca. It was mid-December, a week or so before Christmas, and the ridgetops on Vancouver Island were frosted with snow. Closer to hand, the pallet of a Northwestern winter—the rolling gunmetal gray of the strait, the fingerprint whorls of rain clouds, the somber green of the fir trees and the tawny-colored beach grass—was less festive. Even the river water was a dull, flat sepia color.

But the fish were there, as we had expected.

"There's one," Ron exclaimed, at the exact moment I saw the slash of a trout.

"Definitely a cutthroat," I said.

A second fish broke the surface, then another.

"That was a nice one," Ron said.

For the next 15 minutes, as our street shoes slowly sank into the sodden grass, we watched a small school of sea-run cutthroat work the flooded edges of high slack tide near the creek mouth. We couldn't tell what they were feeding on, but they were definitely feeding. Then, although it was not yet 4 p.m., the early northern darkness began to settle over the strait. It was as though the night was an actual force, crawling out of the earth and grappling with the lowering solstice sky. A band of fog scudded down the strait from the west. In the distance, the basso profundo moan of a ship's horn cut through the enveloping gloom.

"Let's get out of here," I said.

Ron nodded. "We should come back tomorrow, though," he said, as we walked back toward the pickup. "The tide will be perfect if we get here about an hour earlier and fish right up to dark."

"I've got to work," I said. "I've got an article due."

I didn't see Ron again for a couple of weeks, and I forgot to ask him how he did on the estuary. But I have no doubt that he fished the creek mouth the next afternoon. Moreover, I suspect that he has been back to the tidewater pools several times since then and that he now has a wealth of information in the detailed fishing notebook he keeps on his sea-run waters.

As far as Ron is concerned, sea-runs are the most fascinating fish on the peninsula. He fishes for them—and catches them—12 months a year. Indeed, during the long months between the end of the October caddis hatch and the first stirrings of *Callibaetis* on the east side's lowland lakes, when most Olympic Peninsula fly fishers court tendonitis with 9- and 10-weight steelhead rods, Ron and his 4-weight have the creek mouths and estuaries all to themselves. He catches a lot of fish, too.

"I began concentrating on sea-run cutthroat about six years ago," Ron explains. "I was new here and began running into them everywhere—in tidewater and headwaters, in open saltwater and in lakes, in large rivers and creeks. And when I began to study them, I was intrigued by the lack of scientific knowledge about their life histories. I was also fascinated by the fact that coastal cutthroat, *Oncorhyncus clarki*, are the original cutthroat, the progenitor of all the interior races of cutthroat."

Like many of the Olympic Peninsula's most avid and innovative fly fishermen, Ron grew up and developed his fly fishing skills in a different part of the country—along the East Coast and in California, in his case. In early middle age, however, he and his wife Barb sold their carpet business in Northern California and set off in a tiny trailer in search of new home waters. In the course of their journey, they fished for bass in Florida, the fabled streams of the northern Rockies, the Great Lakes and the Mid-Atlantic. But they chose the Olympic Peninsula.

I remember the day I met Ron. It was early fall. Ron had just moved to Port Townsend a few days before, and he dropped by the sporting goods store where I worked. I was sorting topo maps—something I did when I was sick of tourists and salmon fishermen—when I heard one of the other clerks say. "You should talk to Doug. He's the fly fisherman." I turned away from the lovely, green calligraphy of the maps and saw a tall, lanky man approach me. We introduced ourselves and shook hands.

We talked about steelhead first, as fishermen nearly always do when they discuss the Olympic Peninsula. I told him about the Hoko, which was then the region's only catch-and-release fly-fishing-only water for winter steelhead, and I told him how I had taken my first steelhead on a dry fly two summers before on the Sol Duc. Ron talked of the tidal salmon and steelhead rivers of Mendocino County, rivers I had never seen but had read about in Russell Chatham and Dan Blanton's writings.

After a while, the conversation switched to other species, other types of water. I mentioned the peninsula's mountain lakes and beaver ponds and sea-runs. By then, we had the topos spread out in front of us, which have the same pull and solace for sportsmen that rare manuscripts have for scholars. Ron was excited. His eyes sparkled and words gushed from him. I realized that Ron was not only knowledgeable about fly fishing—which is commonplace these days—but that he had a real passion for it, which like all passion, is a much rarer thing. I began to reveal more and more of my favorite locations, something I almost never

did with strangers. By the time he left, I had drawn him a map to my favorite beaver pond.

In the weeks and months that followed, Ron made a point out of stopping by the store and telling me about his exploits. He tried a little bit of everything. But more and more he spoke of sea-runs. His focus were the cutthroat along the gravel beaches and tide flats of Admiralty Inlet and Hood Canal.

"Of all of the species I have fished for, I have never become as enamored of another fish," he says. "Part of it, as I've said, is because you can find them just about everywhere out here that has access to saltwater. They do well in a much greater range of habitat than rainbows. I personally believe that the Olympic Peninsula is the focal point—the center, if you will—of the coastal cutthroat's range."

As Ron learned more and more about sea-runs, he began to linger in the estuaries later and later each autumn, rather than follow the bulk of the run into the rivers. Then, just as Steve Raymond and other Northwestern fly fishermen had done before him, he pushed his sport into actual winter, into December, January and February.

"I asked myself, 'Are some cutthroat in saltwater all year?' By then I had learned that cutthroat cycles are much more irregular than commonly perceived. I knew that individual populations, and even individual fish, can have very distinct habits. For example, I discovered fairly early on that there are two basic life histories for anadromous sea-runs on the east side of the peninsula. There are early returning populations, which are most common on large rivers that have adequate flows during late summer and early fall. But small river cutts often remain in saltwater into winter, waiting for the rains to bring up the creeks.

"Some of the winter fish I took in estuaries, no doubt, were these small stream fish. But I also began to believe that a few cutthroat skipped a year and over-wintered in saltwater. A lot of people were very opinionated on the subject, but my experience had taught me that there is no one answer when it comes to cutthroat life histories."

Ron's intuition, of course, was correct. Indeed, in Pat Trotter's wonderful book *Cutthroat—Native Trout of the West*, Trotter describes how he sent scales from a 20-inch Toutle River sea-run to the Washington Game Department for analysis. The biologists determined that the fish had spent its first two years in fresh water, a typical scenario for sea-runs. But it then stayed two complete winters in saltwater before making its maiden spawning run.

"It was strictly through persistence that I began to take cutts in winter," Ron continues. "Persistence is the most important quality of a winter cutthroat fisherman. Of course, you need to be persistent in all types of fishing. But you need it even more in winter sea-run fishing."

More specifically, Ron believes that each estuary is different. "You have to learn each location separately, because the shape of the watershed influences how the fish respond. Also, cutts will follow bait for quite a distance so you have to know the habits of the local forage species, the candlefish and crustaceans, as well."

As for tackle, Ron's 4-weight is considerably lighter than the rods most estuary fishermen carry. "It's got enough punch to let me cast into the wind," he explains. "But a 12-inch fish in saltwater is a real thrill. It'll really test your rod."

During the winter, Ron usually uses 10-foot, type-3 sink tips. "I like having a long section of floating line," he says. His leaders are six to nine feet long, tapered down to either 4 or 6 pounds. "With the 6-pound tippet I can turn a silver, which I connect with from time to time."

If he were limited to two patterns for sea-runs in estuaries, Ron wouldn't have any trouble selecting them. "My hands down number one pattern is the Bucktail Coachman," he says. "In my experience, red is the color for cutthroat. But it's also

hard to beat a black Woolly Worm or Woolly Bugger." Ron favors smaller patterns. "I fish flies from size 8 on down. I guess my average fly size is a 12. A lot of people say larger flies are preferable, but that hasn't been my experience."

The smallest and least populous Northwestern salmonid, the coastal cutthroat has historically been pretty much an incidental catch on Olympic Peninsula streams. And despite the decline in salmon populations and the increase in fly fishermen in recent years, Ron still has the winter—and even the summer—estuaries pretty much to himself. But he doesn't expect that to last.

"In the future, I think people will come out here specifically to fish sea-runs rather than for steelhead and salmon," Ron ventures. "There are incredible places out here, some of them very obvious if you know what to look for, that are all but overlooked. Also, considering the realities of the commercial and tribal fisheries, whose nets most cutts can safely swim through, and the fact that there is no real commercial significance attached to them for people to fight over, I think cutthroat are destined to become the basic fly-rod fish on the Olympic Peninsula."

Finally, Ron has one other reason he likes fishing for winter cutthroat: It keeps him from having to make the long drive on icy roads out to the West End steelhead rivers.

"You can find saltwater cutthroat within a few miles of every town on the northeastern Olympic Peninsula. I like the fact that I don't have to travel far to get to good winter fishing."

In a place where someone dies in a black-ice-related accident about once a week during cold weather, that is an eminently sensible reason.

I don't like driving on icy roads any more than Ron, but I must admit that I usually only fish estuaries a couple of times each winter. It isn't because of any lack of enthusiasm for the winter cutthroat fishery, though. No, I simply forget about it, succumbing to the steelhead drumbeat that rumbles across the peninsula between December and May.

Each time I have taken a trip to an estuary in winter, however, I have been glad I did. I don't enjoy the success that Ron enjoys, but I have always at least seen fish. Perhaps more importantly, after a steady immersion in winter steelhead habitat, where trees and canyons and rain impose a tight vertical feel, the vast open expanse of an estuary is always exhilarating. I always feel enlivened after a winter day on brackish water, feel that the dull ache of winter has lessened its grip somewhat. Two years ago, for example, I spent a drizzly December afternoon hunting cutthroat on Dabob Bay, a northwestern lobe of Hood Canal. Stretching more than five miles from the tide flats off Tarboo Creek to the tips of the Toandos and Bolton peninsulas, Dabob Bay is the least developed large estuary in Puget Sound. Furrowed slopes heavy with timber rise sharply from narrow beaches littered with drift logs and bleached shell. From most vantage points on the water, the only signs of human activity are a handful of weathered cabins and a couple of mom and pop oyster operations.

I had chosen a mid-afternoon high tide that ebbed slowly into the early winter darkness. As I drove south from Port Townsend, columns of low, gray clouds rolled up from the south. The bay was calm, though, when I launched my boat. I wanted a Dungeness crab for a holiday party, so I dropped a ring trap in the eel grass off a tiny creek mouth. Then I tied a flowing shrimp pattern onto a long leader and played out line until the fly was about 60 feet behind the transom. I pointed the bow toward a large sand spit a mile or so down the bay. I hugged the shoreline as I rowed, obeying the old cutthroat fisherman's dictum to "keep the bottom in sight on the shore side of the boat."

I rowed for more than an hour without turning a fish. Then I saw two swirls a few yards from shore, along the edge of a line of submerged oyster cultch bags.

Quickly picking up my old, fiberglass 6-weight, I retrieved line, then cast a few feet downcurrent of the rises. It occurred to me that the fish could be late-returning Tarboo Creek silvers. But as I stripped the shrimp over the shell bags, one of the fish surfaced again. It was the slashing sort of rise that cutthroat make when they feed on the crustaceans that live on oyster bars, so I was certain they were trout. I worked the area hard for a half-hour, but didn't see another fish, didn't have a strike.

By now, it had begun to rain. Gusts of wind from the south riffled the evergreen leaves on the madronas along the beach, and I could feel the lilting pulse of waves beneath the bow of the boat. Turning around, I saw that small breakers had begun to scroll across the flat windward shore of the spit. I pulled the hood of my yellow foul-weather gear up over my head and cranked in my fly line. I replaced the shrimp fly with a blue-green baitfish pattern, then rowed back and forth across the sloping, submerged tip of the spit. I didn't have a hit.

The wind and rain were even stronger now, and the mouth of the bay was lost in water-level clouds and drifts of rain. I decided to row back to my crab ring and call it a day. The wind was in my face now, and I tilted the bill of my hood down over my eyebrows. Someone had turned the lights on in a cabin on the east side of the bay.

Suddenly, I heard something, something different from the creak of the oar locks and the soughing of the wind across the waves. It was a sound I had never heard before, a tremulous, keening sound. Glancing instinctively toward deeper water, I saw four huge white birds moving slowly toward the head of the bay. They flew in a straight line, only a few feet above the ruffled water. They were trumpeter swans.

I dropped the oars and watched. I watched them until they disappeared into the swirling winter murk. I could hear them for a moment or two after they disappeared. I had forgotten all about trout.

Side channels are important nursery habitat for coho salmon, which spend one year in freshwater before dropping down to sea.

Chapter 19

Winter Lines

For someone who has sold fishing gear for a living, I am a definite tackle primitive. I still use Pflueger reels for everything—brook trout, steelhead, bottom-fish, salmon. The double taper 6-weight that I fish on mountain lakes and sea-runs is 15 years old, while its sink tip counterpart is more than ten years old. I bought my summer-run rod for $75 and two hot Italian sausages at the Tumbling Rapids Campground from a friend who had concluded that he caught more fish and had more fun fishing spinners. The 8-weight I use for winter steelhead and saltwater was left over from the close-out sale at a store where I worked. And my neoprenes were a gift from Ron Link, whom I believe was embarrassed to be seen with someone whose getup looked like a Quilcene chum snagger.

Some of my friends believe that this is posturing, that it is an expression of my contempt for the peculiarly American notion that consumption, competence and experience are somehow synonymous. To a certain extent they're right.

However, economics are the primary reason why I have such a motley collection of gear. To put it bluntly, I don't make a lot of money and I decided a long time ago that I wasn't willing to invest the time that it takes to make more. The way I see it, I would rather fish 10 or 15 times a month with functional gear, than 10 or 15 times a year with snazzy tackle. Also, even when I have money, I tend to travel or buy books, rather than new gear. That doesn't mean I don't appreciate quality tackle. I would love a signature-quality 4-weight bamboo rod for beaver ponds, and there are dozens of stretches of winter steelhead water on the West End that I could cover much more effectively with a Spey rod.

But all I really need to be happy—and what is absolutely essential when it comes to taking winter steelhead—are good lines. Believe me, the finest, most expensive steelhead tackle manufactured won't do you a bit of good if you don't have the appropriate fly line for the water you are fishing. Conversely, you can have a glass rod that throws loops that an elephant could walk through, a no-name reel, a section of mooching leader and a fly from a bubble package and you will do just fine if you have the right line.

"Until the first cold weather comes there will be little sport in Steelhead fishing," Webster quotes C.S. Stakemiller in *Fishing in the Olympics*. "Cold weather means low water and low water uncovers the pools wherein the big fellows are to be found. The principle of the Steelhead game is to cast your bait across the pool and retrieve it near the bottom of the stream. The fish are usually found near the river bed."

A lot has changed in winter steelheading during the three-quarters of a century since Stakemiller uttered those words, but the steelhead that enter freshwater between November and May still spend most of their time within a few inches of the bottom. Good bait fishermen know this and constantly adjust their lead so the eggs or shrimp bounce enticingly along the bottom. So do experienced hardware anglers, who change the sizes and weights of their spinners and spoons to match the water they are fishing. And the fly fishermen that regularly beach winter fish use lines that drag their fly down to the fish's eye level.

Fortunately, such lines aren't hard to come by today. Indeed, there are so many sinking and sink tip lines on the market—some that have been designed specifically for steelhead—a neophyte can easily become bewildered. But anyone that is over 40 can tell you this wasn't always the case. In *Advanced Fly Fishing for Steelhead*, Deke Meyer talks about how Syd Glasso treated silk lines with red lead to get them to sink better. And as recently as the early 1970s, most Olympic Peninsula fly fishermen either relied on full sinking lines or California-inspired shooting heads. The fact that almost no one uses these lines out here today belies the belief that everything was better in the old days.

Over the years, I have interviewed many of the better Olympic Peninsula winter steelhead fly fishermen, along with the most successful local fly fishing guides, and I have always asked them which lines they use for winter fish. The results have been intriguing, to say the least. In the first place, despite the exhortations of line manufacturers and most fly fishing writers, few local fishermen carry more than two types of line. What is even more interesting, however, is the fact that hardly any of these anglers recommend the same lines.

Sink tips, as you would expect, are the overwhelming favorite. But within this broad category just about every sink rate, tip length and brand name has at least one advocate. Moreover, fishermen that specialize in dead-drifting egg patterns or nymphs favor floating lines. Shooting tapers still have a few partisans, especially among anglers who regularly fish deep, far water on the rain forest rivers. And many of the anglers who spend day after day coping with winter flows fashion hybrid lines.

At first, this puzzled me. But I have come to realize that the answer is both simple and obvious: They are all good lines, and in the hands of good fishermen they all take fish.

One of the Olympic Peninsula's most accomplished fly fishing guides, Bob Pigott connected clients with 140 steelhead in 110 days of guiding last winter. Bob uses manufactured lines. "The factories spend a lot of money developing lines," he explains. "It's

hard to beat them at home." His standard line for winter fish is a Scientific Anglers 13-foot sink tip in a Type 4 or 5.

Located atop Gardiner Hill between Discovery Bay and Sequim Bay, Greywolf Angler is the center for fly fishing on the eastern side of the peninsula. Tom Thompson, the shop's proprietor, has wide experience fly fishing on and off the peninsula, in fresh and saltwater. Like Pigott, Thompson fishes Scientific Anglers lines. "I carry a selection of different sink rates," he says.

On the other hand, Ron Link, who in addition to chasing cutthroat has developed a fly fishing education program called the "Fly Fishing Institute," prefers the Cortland 444 10-foot sink tips. "I like the way they handle and shoot line."

In recent years, Teeny lines, which are basically sinking shooting heads fastened to a thick running line, have become popular on West End steelhead streams during winter. And although most anglers fish the lines as they come from the factory, two of the peninsula's most experienced guides customize Teeny lines.

"The T-200 and T-300 are good lines," says J.D. Love, who in addition to guiding on the peninsula also regularly fishes West Yellowstone, Alaska and the Grande Ronde. "But I usually cut them down to about 16 feet."

Herb Jacobsen, another veteran Olympic Peninsula winter steelhead guide, modifies the Teeny lines further. "I usually cut the head back to 18 feet, then splice about 14 feet of 8- or 9-weight floating line between the tip and the running line," he explains. "It picks up and turns better that way."

When the rivers are low and clear in early spring, however, Jacobsen often switches to a dry line. "In April, I fish a lot of surface and subsurface flies on a floating line. I fish little spiders and marabou patterns, usually black with a green butt."

At the complete opposite end of the line spectrum from a floating line, Scientific

Anglers' 550-grain Deep Water Express is the choice of Manual Bernardo, owner of Port Angeles' Quality Fly Fishing Shop. "I use a 17-foot section as a head on the Hoh and Sol Duc, and the remaining 13 feet for the Bogachiel and Calawah. They'll get you right down on the bottom."

For his part, J.D. Love doesn't try to dredge bottom much any more. "I like to fish the lower tidal sections of the rivers for bright fish that are still active and for later-returning wild fish that are really aggressive. All I want is for the fish to be able to see the fly." To accomplish that, he usually fishes a hybrid line on his double-handed rods. "I have a floating line cut back to the belly," he says. "I loop a 12-foot section of Type 6 sink tip to that."

Perhaps because I tend to fish two or three different rivers and several types of water on a typical day of winter steelhead fishing, I carry more lines and tips than most other anglers. I use a 10-foot Cortland sink tip on the higher reaches of the rain forest and Quillayute rivers and on the downstream tailouts when the rivers are low and clear. I have spliced a loop to the end of this line, and when the water is heavier I add sections of sink tips and lead core. This is an idea I got from an article by Lani Waller in *American Angler* a number of years ago. I also carry a floater so I can drift nymphs and large marabou patterns through pocket water or deep runs on rivers like the Sol Duc and Calawah and for the cutbanks, sweepers and shallow water tailouts on Goodman Creek, the Dickey and the Pysht. And I plan to pick up one of the shorter sink tips—I think they are five feet—next winter to use on the faster sections of the smaller rivers.

Despite these idiosyncratic line preferences, I have noticed that nearly all successful Olympic Peninsula winter fly fishermen share a common experience: They put in a lot of hours with drift gear or hardware or plugs before they switched to fly tackle. I don't think this is a coincidence. Indeed, I believe learning how to drift bait through a

tailout or swing a spinner or spoon slowly across the grain of the current is better preparation for winter steelhead fly fishing than decades of warm weather fly fishing. Delicacy of presentation and graceful casting, after all, are much less important in winter than knowing how to set up a swing. And knowing where the fish will hold and how they move up a river is more valuable than all the entomological knowledge in the world when the water is 36 degrees. I've heard more than one guide say that when it comes to winter steelhead they prefer clients with no fly fishing experience to those that have spent years fishing for trout.

Finally, I should mention that nearly all of the West End fly fishing guides now use double-handed rods to propel their winter lines.

"Except for Glo-Bugging on the Hoko, I seldom use single-handed rods anymore for steelhead," says J.D. Love.

Bob Pigott is even more enthusiastic about the long rods. In fact, the license plates on his truck read: SPEY ROD. "If a guy is seriously getting into steelhead or salmon fishing, I personally think he might as well get a Spey rod."

Originating in the same valley in northern Scotland as the celebrated Spey flies, these willowy 14- to 17-foot rods were developed to allow Atlantic salmon fishermen to toss long, roll-type casts on rivers where brush and trees prevented a traditional casting stroke. In North America, Roderick Haig-Brown was probably the first angler to fish for steelhead with a two-handed rod, taking both summer and winter fish from Vancouver Island streams in the 1930s. Spey rods were seldom seen south of the border, however, until the late 1980s.

"Spey rods have two or three advantages," Bob Pigott explained one day, as he, his daughter Erin and I floated the Sol Duc. "For one thing, you can work 60 feet of line at a time, from the tip of the rod all the way to the fly. You don't have to false cast, and you don't have to have your hands up over your shoulders all of the time. For someone like me, whose shoulders are always sore in winter from rowing a boat all day every day, this is a real plus. Also, a lot of older guys can't stand to fish for more than a couple of hours with overhand rods."

"You should get one," he said later, after giving me a crash course in the basic Spey casting stroke.

"I'd like to," I said. "But the whole package costs more than I paid for my truck."

I'm looking for someone who will trade me one for $75 and a couple of Italian sausages.

From the lip of the clay bank, 30 feet above the river, I could see through the soft green water to the bottom of the pool. Three shifting gray shadows played over the gray sand and gravel bottom. They were steelhead, Sol Duc River winter steelhead. More than 20 miles above the mouth, they were in all likelihood native Sol Duc fish. They were also, at least according to statute, safe, because the boundary of the catch-and-release area was four or five miles downstream. With any luck, they would continue upstream, past the fishing deadline at Snider Creek, and spawn in the next few weeks.

Dressed in the austere black, charcoal and pearl of a Northwestern winter, native steelhead show up in Olympic Peninsula rivers much earlier than most anglers believe. The vanguard of the run appears on larger systems as early as late November, about the same time the sea ducks—the goldeneye, bufflehead and old squaws—arrive along the coast. By the end of December, a few wild fish will have nosed up into the lower reaches of even the smaller rivers. And by the time the small streams and the upper reaches of the larger streams close at the end of February, the majority of the steelhead entering the rivers are wild fish.

I had begun the day on the Hoh, hiking through the rain forest to one of my favorite pools at first light. It was the 28th of February, the last day to fish the upper sections of the Hoh, Bogachiel and Calawah. It was also the last day to fish most of the smaller West End steelhead streams. So after a mid-morning sandwich and chat with Gene Owens at the Westward Hoh, I drove down to the Goodman Mainline. I spent an hour fishing Goodman Creek sweepers and cutbanks. After that, I bought a microwave chili dog in Forks, then worked the South Fork of the Calawah for a couple of hours.

By now, it was nearly three o'clock, and I hadn't had so much as a bump all day. I was tired and had those itchy, grainy-feeling eyes that you get when you wake up early and stare at water all day. I pointed the car in the direction of Port Townsend. But the Sol Duc was in perfect shape when I passed the bridge near the ranger station and that made me recall that Bob Gooding had told me there were quite a few bright fish in the middle river. Realizing that I was no longer on my way home, I stopped at the Beaver Store and bought a cup of coffee.

I spotted the three steelhead in the pool beneath the clay bank half an hour later. As I watched the fish measure the current with their pectoral and tail fins, I reflected on how the Olympic Peninsula fly fishing legacy and the struggle to protect wild winter steelhead have always intersected on the Sol Duc. This is where Syd Glasso took his legendary 18-pound winter fish, easily the peninsula's most famous steelhead. A generation later, the Sol Duc was the river where Jeff Cederholm, Hans Norbisrath and other dedicated West End anglers first raised the alarm about hatchery steelhead and overfishing.

More recently, Jim Garrett created many of the patterns that earned him his place beside Glasso in the pantheon of Olympic Peninsula fly tiers when he lived within sight of the Sol Duc. These traditions continue today as the rearing facility at Snider Creek releases native stock Sol Duc smolts into the river each spring and as a new generation of fly fishermen is drawn to the selective fishery water that Bob Pigott fought for on the upper river.

Suddenly, an errant gust of wind riffled the surface of the pool. For a moment, I couldn't see the fish. When the surface cleared, they were skittish, moving about nervously. I waited for them to settle back down, then moved along the top of the bluff into the woods.

Clambering through mouldering, second-growth blowdown, I made my way vaguely downstream. I had worked up a sweat by the time I reached the slight break in the bluff, the spot where the drop is about 10 degrees less than vertical. Thickly overgrown with sword fern and crosshatched by hemlock snags, this is the only place to drop down to the river. I tossed my rod tube ahead of me, then scooted down feet first, using the snapped off limbs of a snag for handholds. Once I stopped sliding, I bucked through a tangle of willow and devil's club to the river.

It's a delicious piece of water, though, well worth the hassle of getting down to it. Upstream, the pool tails out through a boulder field, then falls, foaming and tossing spray, down a rock staircase. The fly water begins just downstream of the whitewater. Between four and six feet deep, with just the trace of a ripple, it glides for 50 yards before widening into a riffle. On the far side, the river is deeper and slower, so it is hard to fish across the faster current lane. But from the rock garden on the shallow side to midstream, it flows slowly and evenly over rock shelves and cobble. The fish hang in the slots between the shelves. When the river is in shape, it carries just the right amount of flow to swing a wet fly slowly, pulsing across the field of a steelhead's vision.

Like all fly fishermen on a stretch of favorite water, I have a ritual for this section of the Sol Duc. I always fish a leech on a sink tip first. I begin with short casts, leading the fly through the pockets at the edge of the rocks. Gradually, I extend the casts until the fly works down and across the shelves on a swing. I slowly fish my way down the run to the head of the riffle, then pick my way back upstream. On my second pass, I fish a weighted Comet, usually a red

one. If I haven't gotten anything by then, I switch over to a floating line and dead-drift a stonefly nymph and a long leader.

I had worked my way halfway down the run when a pair of mergansers appeared from downstream. In the brilliant winter light, their black and white plumage seemed almost too vivid to be real. They followed the exact center of the river, as is their habit. I watched them climb above the cascade, bank around the clay bank, then disappear.

Looking upstream, I thought once again about the steelhead I had seen in the pool. I had told myself that they were safe, free to spawn wherever their instinct carried them. But as I stripped an additional foot of line into my left hand, I wondered about the poachers, the "nobody can tell me where I can fish" guys that flout all restrictive regulations. I also thought about the native steelhead that hadn't made it back to the spawning gravel on the Sol Duc and other Olympic rivers this winter. With all the pressures on them—the tribal netting, the fishermen that keep every fish they catch, the silted-over spawning grounds, the dams and irrigation and homebuilders—I wondered gloomily how they could hold on much longer? It is a refrain that passes through the minds of steelheaders from California to Alaska these days.

But then I thought about a conversation I had with Thom Johnson, a biologist at the Department of Fish and Wildlife's Snow Creek Research Station. For nearly 20 years, Johnson has studied the native winter steelhead and salmon on Snow Creek, a small tributary to Discovery Bay on the Strait of Juan de Fuca. With the information compiled during that time, he and fellow biologist Randy Cooper helped develop the formula the state now uses to determine spawner escapement numbers for steelhead. Johnson was also instrumental in assembling the monumental 1992 Salmon and Steelhead Stock Inventory. When steelhead returns plummeted in 1990-91, Johnson and Cooper analyzed the causes for the crash in "Recent Trends in Steelhead

Abundance in Washington." And recently he helped develop the Genetic Conservation Management Units that the National Marine Fisheries Service will use when it decides whether certain races of steelhead should be declared "endangered." To say that Johnson is one of the most informed people in the Northwest on the subject of steelhead, particularly winter steelhead, is to damn him with faint praise indeed.

Yet, unlike many sportsmen, Johnson is optimistic about the future of the state's native steelhead. He believes the WDFW is on the right track with its Wild Salmonid Policy and Wild Stock Initiative, and he thinks the agency's Steelhead Management Plan will bear fruit. But he also believes that steelhead will ultimately prevail as a species in large part because of their resilience and adaptability.

"Steelhead have a more diverse lifestyle than salmon," Johnson explained. "In any one year, returning steelhead can be from three to six years old and from any one of ten or more brood years. They don't put all their eggs in one basket."

As a result, steelhead stocks tend to survive natural or man-made calamities better than salmon. Consider a mudslide that buries a large number of redds on a small stream. This will obviously have an impact on the number of fish that emerge from the gravel the following spring. For steelhead, however, the effects of the damage will be spread out because the fish whose eggs were destroyed represent a number of different year classes of fish. Moreover, the survivors of the slide will become smolts over a three-year period, which will mix them with juveniles from other brood years. And when they return to the river after one, two or three or more years at sea, the fish will spawn with steelhead from many different generations. In this way, the damage to the run is minimized. Within a few generations, the impact of a bad brood year can be all but erased.

On the other hand, if the same mudslide smothered coho salmon redds, the outcome could be very different. In the first place, coho return uniformly as age groups, usually as three-year-olds. Therefore, virtually all of the eggs that were destroyed will be from one brood year of fish, one of only three that exist on that river. The slide will result in a low number of outmigrating juveniles the following year and, in turn, a significantly reduced run when the adult fish return from the sea. In this way, one bad year can have a dramatic impact on an individual stream's coho salmon return. With the exception of Chinook salmon, most salmon share this rigid reproductive life history. It is easy to see how several bad spawning years, coupled with, say, poor ocean conditions and a high harvest level can send a salmon stock into a population tailspin in a rather short period of time.

Suddenly, a tick on my line snapped me out of my reverie. Setting the hook, I felt something spongy and alive. It was the sensation I had been waiting for all day. For a moment, I was excited. But it wasn't a fish; it was a branch. We all hook them from time to time. They grab your attention for a moment. During the winter they are often the high point of the day. I reeled the three-foot alder branch in and pulled the hook from the bark.

By now, I had covered all of the water I could reach with the leech. It was time to wade back upstream and tie on the Comet. But I was tired—tired of casting, tired of standing in moving water. I also knew that I still had to scramble back up the bluff, work my way through the blowdown and then drive for two hours. I stripped in the line and broke down my rod.

In many kinds of fishing, spending nine hours without a hit would be considered a terrible failure. But in winter steelhead fly fishing this is routine. Indeed, an angler can wait days, even weeks for that electric head shake, that arcing, spray-casting leap. The fish are always there, of course, from before Thanksgiving to the close of the season in April. That knowledge keeps fly fishermen focused. And the strategies, the puzzling over currents and flies and lines, keep anglers busy. But don't let anyone kid you—winter steelhead come hard, often very hard.

"You have really done something when you take an Olympic Peninsula native winter steelhead on a fly," says Bob Pigott. "That is real bragging rights."

Indeed, the peninsula's steep, fast rivers present fly fishermen with even more of a challenge than most coastal rivers. But no other region in the Northwest can match the sheer abundance and diversity of the Olympic Peninsula winter steelhead fishery. For here, on this geologically-tortured uplift, where the heaviest rainfall in the lower 48 states sheds into more than four dozen rivers, winter steelhead encoun-

tered an array of habitat that challenged them like nowhere else. Since the last ice sheets retreated back to the north 12,000 years ago, more than 2,000 generations of steelhead have returned to Olympic rivers. They claimed steep, cascade-strewn rivers. They spawned in dark, brushy creeks. They adapted to rain shadow rivers and rain forest rivers. They even seeded the cloudy glacial torrents that issue from the Olympic's highest peaks. Without any sense of exaggeration, it can be said that here, upon this matrix of lush green foothills, sheared-off submarine peaks and glacier-scoured valleys, the winter race of *Oncorynchus mykiss* reached the ultimate expression of its incomparable biological grandeur.

A Sol Duc River winter steelhead.

Epilogue

The Graywolf River pink salmon had spawned in mid-September, a week or two earlier. Now, hiking the Lower Graywolf Trail, Tim McNulty and I could pinpoint their final resting places without sloshing up the river in waders. We could smell them from the trail.

"There's one around here somewhere," I said, picking up a strong whiff of decaying fish.

"There it is," Tim replied. He pointed at a leeched-out carcass wedged into a streamside root wad.

We were at Two Mile Camp, near the boundary of the Buckhorn Wilderness Area. Originating, appropriately enough, two miles downstream, the Lower Graywolf Trail follows the river for 10 miles to the junction of the Graywolf, Cameron and Grand creeks. Beyond there, the Upper Graywolf Trail extends another 10 miles to Graywolf Pass.

"The fish were still alive when I was here last week," I said.

"How many did you see?" Tim asked.

"Oh, about 70."

Considered a tributary to the Dungeness River, the Graywolf actually drains at least as large an area of the northeastern Olympics as the upper Dungeness. The Graywolf is one of the steepest rivers in North America, dropping nearly a mile in its 25-mile course. Nonetheless, spring Chinook, coho, winter and summer steelhead, Dolly Varden/bull trout and the unique Dungeness "upriver" pinks all historically climbed into the Graywolf to spawn.

Unfortunately, a century of irrigation, logging and development has broken the back of the Dungeness and Graywolf as anadromous fish rivers. Their spring Chinook hover on the edge of extinction.

The rivers' two distinct stocks of pink salmon—the upriver fish that Tim and I saw and a later-timed downstream stock—have declined from runs that numbered in the tens of thousands to a few dozen fish. Not one Dungeness/Graywolf anadromous fish run was listed as healthy in the 1992 Salmon and Steelhead Stock Inventory.

Like many fly fishermen, I had become increasingly worried about the decline of migratory fish on the rivers of the eastern and northeastern Olympics. I was also concerned that the West End rivers' healthy populations of salmon, steelhead and trout were still vulnerable to habitat degradation and overfishing. In an attempt to address these issues, I joined the local chapter of a national anglers' organization and attended meetings of several other fishermen's groups. But I found the endless tackle talk and whining unbearable. And as the threats to Olympic fish became more dire, I decided to talk to someone with a different perspective. Frankly, I wanted some advice.

Tim was a good person to ask. One of the Olympic Peninsula's most respected authors, Tim has published several volumes of poetry, an award-winning series of books on national parks with photographer Pat O'Hara, *Washington's Wild Rivers*, and a new book *Olympic National Park—A Natural History*. In his early years on the peninsula, Tim worked in the woods for a cooperative tree planting and thinning enterprise and in backcountry trail crews in the national park. During all this time, Tim has been a strong, eloquent voice on behalf of the Olympic Peninsula's rivers, forests and wildlife.

"All of the natural resource issues on the Olympic Peninsula—the salmon and elk and old growth—are tied together," Tim explained, after we sat on a rocky knob high above the river. "I lived in the Little Quilcene drainage for a number of years. That area had been hammered by logging in the 1930s. But the railroad logging of those days couldn't get up on the high slopes or down into the canyons. And after 50 years, the areas that had been logged were coming back. It was wonderful walking the old railroad grades and seeing the wildlife and salmon returning to the tributaries.

"But I had a bird's-eye view of logging practices from my forestry work in the 1970s and 80s, and I saw problems," he continued. "The Forest Service began pushing roads into higher, more sensitive areas. The trees aren't growing back in some of these areas. There have been big slides. Spawning and nursery habitat has been destroyed."

I told Tim that I had recently read that run-off from clear-cuts can be nearly twice the volume as in forested areas and that twice the volume creates ten times the force. That much force, the report concluded, destroys redds and fills in pools with silt and gravel.

"There hasn't been as much concern for the health of rainshadow watersheds as there should be," Tim replied. "The East Side rivers are fragile and can't handle the high level of industrial logging as the wetter forests."

For some reason, hearing Tim speak of the East Side rivers made me think of Mount Townsend. Located in the extreme northeast corner of the Olympic Mountains, 6,000-foot Mount Townsend divides the rain and snow that fall on it between the Little Quilcene and Big Quilcene rivers, which flow into Hood Canal, and Silver Creek, a Dungeness River tributary. On a clear day, you can see from the mountain's flat-topped summit across Hood Canal, Kitsap Peninsula and Puget Sound all the way to Seattle. It's a marvelous view, but it is also somewhat unsettling because it reveals just how close the Olympic Peninsula is to the maw of urban America. I mentioned this to Tim.

Tim nodded. "The peninsula's isolation helped shape its unique character and protected it for a long time. But that isolation is a thing of the past. We are plugged right into the mainstream economy now. Many of the big clear-cuts of the 1980s were to finance leveraged buyouts of East Coast companies.

"As resources become scarce, they become more profit-driven," Tim continued. "And as they disappear in other places, more and more people turn to the Olympic Peninsula as a place to make money—or for recreation or to retire. Up to 30 percent of the people in some towns on the peninsula weren't born here. This makes tremendous pressure for development."

"And the timber industry and developers and politicians have become much more effective at exploiting people's economic fears and prejudices," I said. "These days, you can't attend a public meeting without having to listen to someone yammering about the "customs and culture" of the area. One of the customs in the Dungeness watershed was sucking nearly all the water out of the river every summer. That custom is the main reason why there are about 70 pinks in the river now instead of 20,000. And now we have all this talk about the Catron County Ordinance and "county supremacy." If we had county control of the natural resources on the peninsula for the last hundred years, there wouldn't be an elk, salmon or old growth tree left."

Tim nodded. "Local development interests on the peninsula have always run counter to the national interest," he said. "Just look at the sections managed by local government. They are development-driven to the exclusion of trying to protect the resource. Historically, the best management out here has always come from the federal government."

"But there is a concerted effort—on the peninsula and throughout the West—to replace federal control of the nation's public lands with county and state control," I said. "On the peninsula, the battleground is the Elwha. Recently, the dam removal opponents said they wanted the boundaries of the park changed so the upper dam would be outside the park."

Tim grimaced and shook his head. "The fact that a vocal and extremely uninformed minority could have such a negative impact on one of the most significant ecosystem restoration projects in the Northwest is appalling."

Tim and I were silent for a moment. The morning clouds had begun to break up and shafts of sunlight warmed the rocks on the promontory. One thousand feet below us, the Graywolf tumbled noisily down its canyon.

"I used to think—and still do, to a certain extent—that with 900,000 acres in Olympic National Park and 100,000 acres in Wilderness Areas we really didn't have to worry too much. I thought that with the core of the Olympics preserved we were in good shape.

"What I have learned over the years, however, is that the core depends on the health of the peripheral areas. We have seen East Side elk and salmon decline as a result of deteriorating habitat outside the park. Ultimately, the Olympic Peninsula is one single ecosystem. That realization has made me less complacent. And it has made me much more active."

This brought us to the question I wanted to ask.

"In the past, fishermen have tended to undertake stream clean-ups and small-scale enhancement projects when they wanted to help a river or lake," I said. "But it strikes me that this is not really where the battle is being fought today. As much as we may want to shy away from it, fish and habitat are now political issues and that is the arena where their fate will be decided. So how do fishermen, singly and in groups, become a part of this debate. What do we do to make our voices heard?"

It was an unfair question, I realized. But Tim has more experience on natural resource protection than any fisherman I know. He handled it gracefully.

"Well, you can always join an organization and attend meetings. That sort of thing. But from my years of work as a grassroots activist on the Olympic Peninsula, I can tell you that it is amazing how a handful of letters can influence a decision. Environmental groups are always saying 'write, write, write.' But it is really true. When an office gets five or 10 letters, they really pay attention to it. They are our most valuable tool."

"You know, Roy Bergstrom says the same thing," I said. "He is always showing me letters he has written the WDFW or the park or somebody. He says, "It's up to you young guys to do this now. You've got to write letters.""

"Roy's something, isn't he?" Tim said, with a smile. In *Wild Rivers*, Tim had featured Roy in the chapter on the Sol Duc. "How old is Roy now?"

"Eighty-five," I said. "I did a story on him for the Port Townsend paper last year. The week before I talked to him, he had hunted grouse, driven out to the Hoh for steelhead and gone dancing."

Tim and I chatted a while longer, then we shouldered our daypacks and began the easy downhill grade toward Cliff Camp. We found more pink salmon carcasses there and at the bridge just above Sutherland Creek. After lunch at Camp Tony, we hiked back to the trailhead and said good-bye.

The fast way for me to have gotten home would have been to drive down the Upper Dungeness Valley to Highway 101. But the image of the view from Mount Townsend had kept returning to me throughout the afternoon. I turned onto the Forest Service Road 28 and meandered east through the Olympic foothills. A half-hour later, I topped Bon Jon Pass, the divide between the Dungeness and Little Quilcene watershed. I drove down to a spur road that climbs through clear-cuts north of Mount Townsend. There wasn't enough daylight left for a hike to the summit, but I knew a place near the end of the road that also offered an expansive view to the east.

I parked my truck and followed an overgrown skid road into a high elevation clear-cut. For a short distance, the path traveled through young alders and fir trees. Then the route traversed a steep slope. The ridge climbs sharply above here, a tangle of silvered slash and fireweed. Looking the other direction, I could see the gray tide flats of Quilcene and Dabob bays and the long blue arm of Hood Canal. In the hazy autumn distance, I could see Seattle.

It is always a little disorienting, standing on a windswept ridge, many miles from the nearest human being, and looking at the dirty white roof of the Kingdome, the vertical gray spires of the downtown office buildings. After all, cougars and black bears wander these hills and draws every night. Blacktail deer and grouse live their entire lives within a square mile or two. Yet within the paltry reach of a human being's vision, rise the edifices of the Northwest's largest city. It doesn't take much imagination to smell the exhaust of transit buses and hear the keening of sirens.

From this aerie, it is possible to see both the dilemma and the promise of Olympic Peninsula salmonids. For here, where a metropolitan skyline and the ragged, tidal edge of the peninsula's eastern boundary are visible in a single glance, is where the juggernaut of American commerce and industry has piled into the last relatively intact, large anadromous fish ecosystem in the lower 48 states. And although the cold-water fisheries of the peninsula are in much better shape than any comparable area south of Alaska, the Graywolf and Dungeness are not the only stocks of salmon, steelhead and trout to have declined in recent years.

"It's the Indians and the seals," choleric voices sputter.

"There were plenty of fish when only Indians and seals were here," more temperate voices counter. "It's habitat degradation and overfishing."

Still others blame "El Niño." Or the Japanese. Or the Canadians. Or all the damn guides.

Ironically, E.B. Webster, whom I have quoted so freely on these pages, knew what the problem was more than 70 years ago.

"...back in the early '90s, when fishermen were few and trout practically unlimited in number, when salmon ran in countless millions and were brailed from traps in bargeloads, when canned fish, even in the central states, was a drag on the market at ten cents a pound—in those days great catches were made.

"Now, with fleets of skiffs and summer resorts all around the shores of the lakes and with camping parties every half mile along the Highway, fishing isn't what it used to be..."

Indeed, every single difficulty that Olympic Peninsula fish face today can be traced back to one source—human beings. Logging, irrigation, hatcheries, dams, pollution, development, overharvest—all of these activities damage fish. They also all benefit people, at least some people. And as the number of people that live and visit the peninsula increases, the pressure on the remaining Olympic fish and their habitat increases steadily. As Tim McNulty said, we are plugged into the mainstream today.

Actually, the peninsula was never really as remote as its residents and the people that visited wanted to believe. Loggers stripped the lowland forests near deep water ports like Port Ludlow and Port Crescent during the late nineteenth century. Market and subsistence hunters nearly wiped out the Olympic elk herds by the turn of the century. And pound net operators, irrigators and dam builders destroyed entire runs of salmon.

To get a grasp of how dramatically the distance between the skyscrapers of Seattle and the aerie above Deadfall Creek has shrunk in recent years, all you have to do is shorten your gaze from the city to Hood Canal. Fed by steep, glacial rivers and tangled, short-run streams, the canal's eel-grass flats and clam beds were once one of the most robust salmon, steelhead and sea-run cutthroat nurseries in the Northwest. Until the 1960s, as many as 40,000 summer chum salmon returned to the canal every year. Pink salmon swarmed up the Dosewallips, Duckabush and Hamma Hamma sometimes more than 200,000 fish in a good year. Spring and fall Chinook, summer and winter steelhead, sea-run cutthroat—the canal hosted every species of North American Pacific anadromous fish save sockeye.

"I used to drive down to the Dosewallips from Port Townsend and fish for winter steelhead," Roy Bergstrom recalls. "The limit was three fish then, and I'd usually have my fish before noon. Then I'd drive over to Black Point on the canal and fish for blackmouth from my pram. I'd get a limit of them, too."

In 1994, sport fishermen took three steelhead from the Dosewallips during the entire month of January. But that is far from the worst news on the canal. The spring Chinook and pink salmon of the Skokomish River, the canal's largest, are extinct, the victims of a hydropower dam and poor logging practices. According to Nehlsen, Williams and Lichatowich's paper in the American Fisheries Society journal, overfishing by commercial fishermen and introgression by hatchery fish, have reduced the summer chum population to less than 1,000 fish. Similarly, chronically low spawner escapement by wild Hood Canal coho in recent years has been one of the principle reasons for the summertime salmon closures on the Strait of Juan de Fuca and Puget Sound in 1994 and 1995. Even sea-run cutthroat, the once nearly ubiquitous tidewater trout of Hood Canal's oyster bars and creek mouths, are now listed as "of special concern" because of habitat degradation, overfishing and competition from hatchery fish.

But if people are the problem facing the Olympic Peninsula fish—they can also be the solution. It wasn't divine intervention—or the tender mercies of the market economy—that saved the peninsula's Roosevelt elk, glaciers and rain forests, after all. It was turn-of-the-century explorers like Lt. O'Neil and James Wickersham, who returned from the Olympics with recommendations for a national park. It was German immigrant pioneer and forest reserve employee Chris Morganroth, who traveled to Washington D.C. to speak for the creation of a park in the Olympics. It was courageous politicians like congressmen Francis Cushman and Mon Wahlgren, who stood up to the timber barons and chambers of commerce. And it was the two Roosevelt presidents—Theodore, who created the Mount Olympus National Monument in 1909 to save the elk and Franklin, who signed the bill that created Olympic National Park 29 years later.

Unfortunately, anyone who reads the newspapers can tell you these aren't good times for either the creatures or the stewards of our wilderness. Today powerful Western senators scheme to allow unregulated logging, and to make grazing and mining on public land easier and cheaper. Ignorant rednecks harass and intimidate government biologists and rangers, often with the blessing of county officials. And today the war cry of "customs and culture" reverberates as ominously for the surviving wildlife and plants of the American West as "Manifest Destiny" did for the buffalo and First Nations people a century ago.

That is why this is the time for anglers that love the Olympic Peninsula's wild fish to make their voices heard. This is the time for a renaissance of activist visionaries like the ones that created the Olympic National Park and saved the elk. With most of the spawning grounds of the larger rivers in the national park—and more than 70 percent of the peninsula public land—it can truly be said that these magnificent fish are held in common by us all. Those of us that live here can attend the meetings and work in the political trenches. But anglers in Seattle and Portland, Chicago and New York, can also become an important part of this struggle for the price of a stamp. Indeed, one intelligent, reasonable letter to the administrator of an agency or a politician can carry more weight than a dozen people yelling at a public hearing.

So when I look east from Mount Townsend these days, I see solutions as well as problems. And I am hopeful.

A fly fisherman with a good pair of hiking boots can find breath-taking scenery, wild fish and—perhaps its ultimate treasure—solitude in the Olympics.